34 Steps to Lose Yourself

34 Steps to Lose Yourself

PULKIT HEERA

PARTRIDGE
A Penguin Random House Company

To order additional copies of this book, contact
Partridge India
000 800 10062 62
orders.india@partridgepublishing.com

www.partridgepublishing.com/india

AND, THE NOMINEES ARE……………….

I.	THE NAGGING QUESTIONS	17
II.	WHO IS GOD?	24
III.	WORDS ARE ALL I HAVE	32
IV.	IS MY BRAIN, MY ENEMY????	35
V.	IS MY BRAIN, MY BUDDY????	43
VI.	THE SOCIAL NETWORK………… REALLY????	46
VII.	THE SOCIOBRATS- "A MOCKUSCRIPT"	50
VIII.	MY GAME, MY RULES	58
IX.	RELATIONSHIPS 101	66
X.	COMMITMENT PHOBIA	71
XI.	TYPES OF LOVERS- "THE PRAYING MANTIS"	75
XII.	FINALLY, 'THE PRAYING MANTIS'	84
XIII.	'THE COMPROMISER' AND 'THE COMPROMISEE'	89
XIV.	"FINALLY, THE PRAYING MANTIS …………." CONTD.	93
XV.	TYPES OF LOVERS- 'THE GRASSHOPPER'	95
XVI.	ARE YOU GOOD AT FAKING IT????	102

XVII.	EXCUSE ME! WHERE CAN I FIND HAPPY????	106
XVIII.	YOU'RE HONOR, I OBJECT!!!!!!	113
XIX.	NEGATIVE HAPPINESS? THEORY OF ADSORPTION	118
XX.	HEART: *"WHY DO YOU ALWAYS BLAME IT ON ME?"*	125
XXI.	HAVE FUN WHILE YOU CAN	129
XXII.	TAKE A DAY OFF	135
XXIII.	WHAT DO I DERIVE, WHEN I DRIVE????	142
XXIV.	BRAND GOD: RELIGION INC. PVT LTD.	149
XXV.	GOD FOR SALE	153
XXVI.	THE GREAT INDIAN ARRANGED MARRIAGE BAZAAR	157
XXVII.	THE RENDEZVOUS	162
XXVIII.	THE INDIAN LOVE MARRIAGE	166
XXIX.	I'M IN LOVE AND MY PARENTS DUNNO	169
XXX.	DO YOU HAVE THE SE"X" FACTOR????	178
XXXI.	HAVE WE ALWAYS BEEN SEXISTS????	188
XXXII.	IS GOD A WOMAN????	193
XXXIII.	BIG BOYS DON'T CRY	197
XXXIV.	ROLL SOUND, CAMERA………...ACTION!!!!	201

For Mum and Dad

They call it "Preface" or "Prologue"
Actually, it is "A heads up on what you're getting into"

HEADS UP

So, you have decided to pick up this copy and intend to go ahead with it. As the author it is my duty to give you a synopsis of what you are getting into. Actually it contains no heavy stuff that may be dreaded. Through this medium we are about to have a conversation. A simple, basic chit-chat about stuff. From what I see, we have had enough of rules, lectures and discourses in our lives. We have been told by loads of supposedly smarter people, what to do and how to make our lives better. Guess what? Our lives are the best they could be. We don't need another Life coach, navigating us through its twists and turns. The need that is needed is the need for a conversation. An honest, 'heart to heart' is what we need to make everything alright. So come, let's chat. Let's sit down with our steaming coffee mugs (or any beverage you prefer) and do something we did not have to learn about at school. Talk from our hearts. That is what we are about to do now.

We shall have snippets of conversations whenever our schedules permit.

(*Disclaimer: You do not need to read this book back to back; just pick it up whenever you feel like and then put it down*).

We shall talk about any random topic that comes to our mind whenever we please.

(*Disclaimer: Flip through, pick any page, no need to be bound by chapter rules*).

Sharing is best for both joy and grief. Multiplies the former and diminishes the latter.

What are we planning to talk about? Almost everything that can fit in a regular sized book. Those questions and situations which creep up at irritating junctures and demand our attention. Topics that make gossips juicier. Topics like- Relationships, link-ups, break-ups, soul mate, Women, God, Prayer, Truth, Life, Sex, Movies, Road, Traffic, happiness.................... the usual stuff conversations are made of. Don't worry, we shall not go anywhere you lose your depth. We shall keep it simple. A footnote here and there. We shall do what friends do. I have outlined the usual kind of problems you may be facing, or I faced in the past. Take it as a pep talk, a 'pick me up' or counseling.

Wisdom. The dictionary meaning of this word is- "*The quality of being wise. The quality of having experience, knowledge and good judgment*". This is something we gain throughout life. It tells us what is right and what wrong. But, is it mandatory that whatever has been spoon fed to us as being right until now is right? Can it not be wrong? Is not one man's right, other man's wrong. Look at something from here and it seems right. Change your position and it may start appearing wrong. Better not to get into the squabbles of right and wrong. They only cause stress. Let's define our own 'rights' and 'wrongs'. Those 'rights' and 'wrongs' which have nothing to do with the typecasts. Probably the wisdom that has been pumped into you for years, may actually have been Wis"dumb". You never know.

Now let us give a name to the type of this book. This book is a .... I'm sorry. I am at a loss to tell you exactly what this book is? It does not fit into any particular, tailor made genre. It is not fiction, so it must be non-fiction. The fun part is that it is not self help, philosophy, comedy, satire, personality development or any such type. So, what shall you gain after reading it? I would say- trust me, go ahead and you tell me what genre this book belongs to. We shall create a genre of our own. Is that not what we all should do? Do not get into the rat race. Don't be- *"I'll do what my father did and he did what his father did"*. Make your own rules, play by those and excel.

Learnt enough? Now start un-learning. Lose the usual, the common, the mundane, the boring and the normal. Lose yourself. Get on these steps and you shall start dispelling the illusion with each step, one by one until you reach the 34th. You need to lose yourself, to find the real you. Un-learn to learn and lose to find.

Shall we start then? Tell you what; let's start off by breaking stereotypes. Let's chat about the most controversial thing at the very beginning. Let's explore the taboo, delve into it, turn it around and un-taboo it. This is the way it's gonna be.

HOW TO MAKE A BILLION

I'm sorry but the book hasn't started yet. I was just yanking your chain. This is not the first chapter. I am not here to fool you with quack nostrums, so this will not be the type of matter you find in this book.

This POST-PROLOGUE passage is just a reality check.

They say that the best things in life are for free. Guess what? They lie. There is no such thing as free on this earth. The joke is that the thing which is called free is generally the one which cannot be bought. Top of the list comes- Free Will. The will of someone else to go by your will. No amount of money in the world can buy Free Will. So how come it is called Free?

We end up paying for everything, regardless of the fact whether we pay in cash or some other way. These other ways are the most scary. When we make mistakes and gain experience, that experience does not come for free. It comes for a price. We all do pay the price (*generally against our will*) but still, things don't go our way. How come some of us have everything going their way? Why are some of us able to achieve what they want, when they want?

Actually, there are certain cheat codes. Life is like an untamed beast. If you know how to put a leash on it, it can be domesticated as per your whims. Untamed, it becomes a predator. The only trick is to do this as subtly as possible. Just change your perspective of looking at things. Turn your life around. Find its weak spots and dig your spurs into its sides. Then it shall do what you tell it to do.

Life is beautiful. The only trouble is the way we look at it. We see it through a dull point of view. Let us try to look at it through a tilted angle, a different perspective. I am sure it shall amaze us. Life is fun, when we see it upside down. Ever tried standing on your head and looking around, topsy-turvy, with the blood gushing to your head. That is fun. Everything appears weird, but strangely amusing. That is what has to be done (*only occasionally*).

Now the question arises- how to explore this different perspective? It begins with breaking stereotypes and myths. Getting the true and real picture and stumbling on to some secrets. To change the way you think, do not follow the herd. Do something exceptional and excel in it.

Let me share a few secrets I have stumbled on to. Let's talk business. Let's change the way you think.

I

THE NAGGING QUESTIONS

All the texts containing THE wisdom, the light, the key, the truth; the various texts in various religions, so called religions, the sayings, the quotes, speeches by the enlightened, the Godly, the powerful, the saints, the educated, the self proclaimed Gods or agents of God.........................pheww; have a multitude of versions, distortions, amendments, translations, adaptations but, the TRUTH is One, single, irrefutable and timeless.

For those of my readers, who have not the gift of patience here is a gist of this tardy paragraph: All throughout the universe The Truth is One unanimously agreed upon; only the ways are different, destination the same.

So where is this truth? Is it a part of knowledge that has been lost? Alarming concept isn't it? It is so arduous to gain knowledge, to collect it, that after such labor, losing it is quite a bummer. So, what is this knowledge that has been lost? And how do we know that it actually is lost. Are we sure it ever existed? When we, are not even sure of it being present in the first place, how can we say it is lost? Difficult to digest but true.

This is occurring everyday in this world, all the time. Though enmeshed in our everyday lives, we still have many nagging questions at the back of our mind. We crave the answers of our being- *why, what is our purpose, since when, how, till when.............?*

This is not some propaganda of conspiracy theorists or mystery hunters. Ancient texts and wisdom speak of existence of some knowledge present in a human brain throughout, since the time of birth. This knowledge is supposedly locked, but resides in everyone deep within the subconscious. It is perhaps covered by multiple veils, which can be removed layer by layer, by only proving your worth. Haven't all of us, wondered at least once in our lives, what do the babies think? What goes on in their tiny brains? What thoughts cross their gray matter? If babies could speak, what would they say? If we could interpret the waves of their brain (*actually we can do that*) and convert them into coherent sonic signals (*sadly, this we can't do*) what fascinating secrets would spill out.

Sounds like an '*Indiana Jones*' movie, but the echoes of this theory have been found in various nooks of history. Man does possess supernatural powers and knowledge, but has forgotten or never knew in the first place how to use them.

Coming back, The Truth, the answers to our nagging questions have always been in front of us, to be seen, the whole time. Truth is simple, contrary to what the indefatigable fantasies of its seekers concoct it to be. It has always been here, in front of our eyes, waiting to be experienced, not even discovered or uncovered or decoded. No. God is kind. She/He didn't wrap the truth under some mysterious symbols or veils of mysteries so that it could be unraveled one day by some super intelligent hero or some great enlightened soul or a seer and to be disseminated amongst Us the common ignorant masses. Each one of us is perfectly capable of discovering it. So where does the problem lie?

We have become materialistic and prefer everything to be decorated, packed and presentable. We expect thousand and one things due to our weakness for the dazzling and glamorous. A great find in simple packaging ceases to impress us. That is how the super power plays. Life is the biggest enigma of the human mind. We have an endless thirst of not what is out there but of what is in here.

The questions are asked and the answers are given but those answers do not satisfy us. The daily gruel prevents us from getting closer, from distinguishing fact from fiction and even if we do, there is a suspicion. Is what we believe to be fact, really fact and what we discard as fiction, thus? Might it not be vice versa and if it was, then whatever we have based our beliefs on, seems pointless. God equipped each and every one of us with the vision to see the truth, the senses to experience it, the heart to enjoy it. But like everything it comes with * Conditions Apply. These conditions are- Free Will. Yes, as simple as that.

We do not need to meditate for 1000 years in a cave to know the basic truth. By this I mean no disrespect for those great sages who toil with great tolerance, humility and faith in search of God and enlightenment. Those are the real ascetics, the real workers of God; they can be, by no means belittled. They spend their lives in anonymity for the goal to being One with the Almighty.

But we do not covet those goals. We the materialistic people who are very happy with our fast lives infused with technology. We do not desire to know any more, than we already do. But, despite being embroiled in the cobwebs of our everyday lives, despite being stuck in the nets of occupation we created ourselves, we do feel. When we sit back, when we can't think any more, when we 'Space Out' (*excellent term, I find this singularly applicable to our lives*), when we are thinking without thinking, thus when our sub-conscious takes over and pushes the day to day problems away from the spotlight. That is when we feel it. The craving, the unquenchable thirst. The nagging feeling that something is missing. Something is not right. That, we need to know something. Something that is so close within our reach yet so elusive. This is the basic and primordial longing for truth. The Truth.

This longing has been inculcated in the very existence of human ever since human is known. It exists in us or rather we exist in it. For the more scientifically bent minds it is present in some undiscovered segment of our DNA. We want to know.

Do we not wonder occasionally, if we sit and think how come the man is aware and almost sure of certain things, when there has never been any formal discourse of such knowledge at any point of time? Not through a book, a prophet, a teacher, a figure or likewise.

Yes, we are aware of certain things without being aware as to the source of this awareness. We can argue that the knowledge, the answers to all unsolved questions, the keys to all bolted doors are present inside us. All the ciphers exist along with their solutions in our conscious. We just do not always find them. Either we don't bother, or we don't have a pressing urge to find the answers for the simple fact that most of us are not henpecked by these questions.

We are involved in our daily lives. Work, family, comforts, luxuries. We have been entangled in their snare such, that it is a mammoth task to lift above the mundane and seek the Truth. Yes, we do find this written in sacred texts and also in the discourses of Prophets. They call it the illusion. We are trapped in an illusion which keeps us busy and to some extent satisfied by producing minor problems and seeking solutions. We find solutions for these trifling issues and enjoy the whiff of complacency; never realizing that we are being subjected to what is called, being underplayed. We are being forced to use our faculties to sub optimal levels for trivial issues which actually don't matter. We are being forced into a shell and prevented from reaching, even discovering our true potential.

Thinking
    Instincts
        Criticism
            Self assessment
                Hundreds of waking hours
                    Reading of scriptures, spiritual texts

These are the weapons, to name a few which people endow them with, to reach the truth. But as I said earlier the truth is simple, unadorned, honest, straight forward without any artificial decoration.

COUNTER POINT

The human being is capable of magnanimous feats which are far beyond making billions, ruling the world or being popular. But is it actually so important? Many would argue that they are happy this way. Why should I run after some fantasy truth when I am happy and content with what pursuits I already possess? Family, education, business, money, these things are of paramount worth too. I derive pleasure and satiety in the struggle for these goals. Why should I forego these for some so called Mythical intrigue for the truth, the quest for enlightenment? As long as I do my work honestly I don't see any reason that it is insignificant. I am happy. I have material and spiritual means to please me. I am at peace when I achieve something. So thank you but I have all that I need to be going and I don't need any fanciful voyage of Sinbad into my subconscious to unlock the mysteries of the universe.

Fair point.

I have no answer at all. No contradictions, no argument which may deter this school of thinking. If there really was some hidden truth it wouldn't have been under so many veils and curtains. It would have been more apparent. Like the other more apparent truths such as- the need for love, education, money. These are all very clear and approachable, unlike this fabled Eternal truth.

But even as I write I find my disagreement mounting by the minute. However much we may contradict or suppress our instincts, the urge remains. There is more to what we know. There is more to what meets the eye. We are powerful beings. Each one of us contains a portion of the Creator. In fact all of us together, combined, joined, fused comprise the Creator.

We are using only subtotal levels of our faculties. For the skeptics a medical man would confirm that humans use only 30% of their total cerebral capacity aka brain. A patient under the influence of an Epileptic seizure unleashes tremendous energy and vitality which seems impossible in the normal state. Not going too far, even a paroxysm of emotions- rage, bliss, grief enable a man to unlock supreme physical and mental energy and perform tasks which stem astonishment.

Where does this power come from and where is it hidden? Or is it never hidden? It lays waiting to be summoned. Only we are unaware of the correct way to summon it. At times when we are not brutally conscious as always, some mechanism falls into place, like the correct gears locking in and release this energy. We have experienced it. Each one of us. Should we choose to ignore it at our own loss, none is to be blamed. But should we choose not to ignore, that presents to us a deeper thought to delve into.

II

WHO IS GOD?

There are a million and one questions in our mind, but not one as strong and as irritating as- Who is God? The One, The Creator, The Big Guy. Is God a She or a He? (*I believe God is a She. We shall discuss this at length in "Is GOD a Woman????"*)

Is She/He someone with an actual form and face? Does She/He have a body? Is God somewhat similar to the imaginatory fellow seen in our movies? A big booming voice emanating from someone, who is obscured by white fog, wears white robes OR is decked up with ornaments, Gold crown, equipped with all weapons imaginable, with many hands and many faces.......................Which version of God is true? Which religion has described the Guy (or Gal) accurately and most closely? What to believe? Is it just a phenomenon? Just a belief? A symbol of faith? Does God actually not exist, as in does not exist in flesh and blood? Maybe She/He is just an Energy source? Something or someone who provides unlimited power constantly and runs this whole Game. Or is God an element?

Generations of believers have made us to believe in God. It has become our second nature. A spinal reflex- to believe in God, to fear God. The father and mother taught their son and/or daughter to believe in God and so they believe in God. No one dares to question the authority, lest some misfortune befalls. So, we pray, seek, give ourselves up. Why then are we still not happy? Why do we have to experience grief, loss, desperation and agony? The most repeatedly and aggressively expressed allegation in the World probably would be-

"God doesn't listen to me" or the more formidable version "God hates me".

Saying this provides us with a kind of savage and grim satisfaction which comes with challenging the authority. Also it is somewhat akin to the self flagellation routine practiced by orthodox Catholics. While they inflict physical injury, this is inflicting emotional trauma. We have lots of complaints with God and that is the main reason we want to find Her/Him. Give her/Him a piece of our mind. ☺ :D

Jokes apart we all have this grudge at some point in our lives. Why am I not happy? Why has God abandoned me? Why does She/He pile trouble upon trouble in my life? Why is my life a glorified spectacle of agony? Why does God test my patience and faith so much? (*This next is my favorite*) What did I do to deserve this? I am a good human being but I have seen those who are rotten and still being showered with all that is beautiful and desirable on this earth.

It would be a white lie to say that even one of us has never felt this way at some point of time. For some it has almost become a daily recital instead of a humble prayer. Where is this God and how to reach Her/Him? Do our prayers really make any impact in any way? Do they really affect the ongoing tides of time and modify the course of our lives? Is praying to God of any use?

They say that everything in this world is pre-destined. Our lives are webs and the world is an intricate sphere of these interconnected webs. Each human being affects every other being in a positive or a negative way. Though the quantum of influence varies depending on the physical proximity. So if everything is already decided by destiny or to put in a more sophisticated fashion- 'All is pre-ordained', what is the use of a prayer? When the course of life has been engraved with the twists and turns through bliss and grief will a human's prayer, when she/he is in grief make any dent.

If what has been said is believed, it won't. they say that, nothing can alter the divine plan. So why do we pray, and where is this God to whom the prayer is addressed? Does the mere folding of hands or looking up to the heavens direct these prayers to the right address? When we don't have the shadow of a clue as to where the Creator resides, how do we pray, and if we do will this prayer be actually fruitful? I do not know. These questions plague me as much as they do to any with reasonable mental faculties.

Following is what I believe in.

The creator is not a body, the picture we amuse ourselves with and which is imprinted in our minds. Though there is nothing wrong with that. As long as we reach the destination, it is immaterial what path we took. God won't mind in what way we imagine Her/His appearance to be. The truth, as I believe is that God does not have any shape or size.

God is an infinitely powerful source of energy, a burst of force which needs to be contained. The force has to be disseminated in order to create and construct. Concentrating the energy would have led to destructive results (it actually does in the shape of-apocalypse, judgement day, armegeddon, pralaya.......so on). Such a powerful source of energy can create and sustain as easily as it can annihilate.

The power used for Creation and Destruction is the same, only the application is different. Creation and destruction are the cycles. The cycles that have been mentioned in the ancient wisdom of all modern day religions. Life is created and then it is destroyed, paving way for a fresh start. This huge unlimited focus of energy called God, needs to be divided and disseminated into multiple small reservoirs. This is done so that it can sustain. Hence the reservoirs are created. The energy is divided into and contained in billions and billions of pockets of minute reservoirs of energy.

The God who was One now becomes billions. All these reservoirs collectively can be termed as God. We are these reservoirs. By 'We', I mean all the living and breathing creatures. We all are the small packets of energy, each having received a fragment from the main source. All the beings who move, breathe, procreate do this by the energy from the main source. When a reservoir or a shell containing the pocket of energy wears out, it disintegrates. The calculated quantum (amount) of energy escapes and fuses into the main source, whence it may be infused into a fresh shell and restart its journey. Sound familiar or too much of physics????

It is all accurate though. This is what all the religious texts and scriptures say. God is not up above in the heavens or in deep sea. God is and has been here. Always and steadfast. This main source of energy is called God, the reservoir is the Body and the packet of energy is called Soul. When a person dies (the shell wears out) the soul escapes and becomes one with the Almighty. The reincarnation theory states that this soul now assumes a different body and commences its cycle again. Also, it is believed and repeated that God lives in each one of us. How else can we explain this?

Yes, God truly does reside in us, because the source of energy which resides within us, the tyke we know as Life is actually a fragment of God. God's particle. Each one of us is God's particle. So, God does reside inside us. The day we are born till the day we die, God lives with us in this very body.

The body which enables us to the sins of vanity and pride. We never had the need to look out. No need to search for The Almighty in the rocks, mountains, deserts, seas or the sky. No need to make arduous journeys to nowhere to bow down to the Holy. We are Holy. God is inside. We just need to clean out the grime of self importance and try to listen to the feeble sounds which are actually the voices of our heart.

All answers lie within (lie as in lay, not the lie that means not true). The questions are easier to find but the answers have been engraved into the various layers of our conscience. It is up to us to go as deep as we can delve. Sitting with one's self, talking to one's self can reveal all that one ever wanted to know, or the knowledge shall ever require. It is us. We are proof. Proof that God exists. Because we exist. Our existence is a testimony to the presence of the Almighty.

FREE WILL

God always shows us a way which eventually leads to a fork. We have to choose, which path to pursue. We always have a choice. Our Destinies are not laid out by God. She/He gives us free will to choose our own destiny. Free will. The myth, that God has already created a map for our lives or a game plan or has decided each and every second of our lives from the day we are born to the day we die, is a little indigestible. Everything is planned???? I don't believe it.

THE MYTH

They say that every breath we inhale, every step we take, every motion our body executes is already written, or carved in stone or kept in some USB drive for that matter :P. This means, that whatever joys and grief we have to experience in a lifetime must also have been decided by the creator? Thus, it is God only who makes us happy and sad by providing respective circumstances? No matter how we lead our lives, how much good or wrong we do, whether we are a scoundrel or a philanthropist, whether we are a saint or a cut-throat, it has already been decided? Does this mean, that the way we lead our lives has no reflection on the fruits we bear? Someone may spend all her/his life being kind and good and may suffer from unending woes? Then vice versa should also be true.

I find this theory to be cowardly. This means, that we are not ready to take the responsibility of our actions. We are not to own up, but just blame God for everything wrong that happens. An assassin may claim, that it is not his fault that he paints his mugs with peoples' blood now and then. It is a divine decree. It is how God has made him. So, the assassin is not answerable for his deeds? The blood of what might be, a multitude of victims is God's problem. Isn't this blatantly erroneous? I have never heard a more cowardly statement. If I may (*pardon my language*) this is utter Bullshit!!!!!! with a capital B.

We all know we have free will. When a decision comes up, God does not force us to go a certain way. We are merely provided with all the data and the pros and cons. We are gifted with intelligence, insight and morals. God lays out pathways and turns and conditions. According to the circumstances, our mind gives us options. These options are weighed, but it is totally our sweet decision on what to do. Whether to listen to our conscious or strangle it? Lots of factors come into play at such a time. Righteous has to combat with Wrong. An internal struggle takes place. It seems very agreeable to give in to the easier and generally the negative emotions. Avarice, self, cowardice, malice, jealousy are some of the friends who rule. Generally they only decide our course of action. The course as we may imagine is ultimately the wrong one. We take the wrong door, the wrong exit and end up in mire. Then we have to face the music. No one likes that. And it becomes joyfully easy to blame and abuse God for everything.

"God only made me do that back then
and see now what has happened"
"God hates me. Loves to see me rot in this living hell"

How often have these assortment of words tumbled out of our mouths? I confess, I have uttered these very words many, many times in my short life. Everyone has. It feels good, gives us a morbid kind of enjoyment and contentment. However good may it feel, it is wrong. Aaaeeeennnnn. Wrong answer. Wrong, wrong, wrong. Just flash back and remember. At every decision in your life, immaterial of whether it turned out to be Gold or Dung, you had a choice. We always have a choice and free will.

Our lives are not like those 80s video games with a set closed pathway, where you have to play and you cannot wander away anywhere. God has not laid down a closed and barricaded road map for us. She/He has opened a world for us and given us a choice. In the end how our lives turned out to be, depends on us. The onus as they say lies on us. God is the master but has not enslaved us. She/He watches her circus from the sidelines. She/He created us, gave us options and lets us free. Then She/He sat down and now observes as to what we make of our lives and of the world She/He introduced us into. At times She/He may give a slight push or jolt, here and there but that's that. She/He does not make our decisions for us and definitely does not spoon feed us.

Sometimes it appears like a mammoth experiment or a science project. God is the scientist and we are the guinea pigs. (*Ok, that was a horrible metaphor*). But is not this idea revelatory to a certain extent. We should start or at least start to learn taking responsibilities of our actions. Shoulder our burdens. Enough of escapism. The blame game does not always work. And it certainly fizzles if we are blaming God. You cannot give a hard time to the One who taught you how to give a hard time.

III

WORDS ARE ALL
I HAVE.............................

Words. The ultimate enigma of Mankind. When they say the pen is mightier than the sword they are not joking. Though, some of my peers who possess more machismo may not agree and desire to break my wooly head, it is true. Words change destinies of people, groups, communities, nations even the whole world. Words are powerful. The most basic and yet the most potent and volatile weapon bestowed on the mankind. Words are like recipes. Concocted correctly they can win the world for you. The right mix, proportions, ratios served forth, at the perfect time have turned paupers to rulers. Of course, these are double edged swords as well. Improper use is hazardous and unfortunately now days, often we are subjected to horrendous experiences in our lives, which are an off-spring of erroneous application of the word power. It is fun, to play with words. The diplomats, who serve, as extremely vital cogs of the government machinery and who build the face of a whole nation, are the ones who are gifted wizards of word play. They are living examples, who will attest, that the most monumental decisions which affect the lives of millions, are reached upon, by skilled and tactical word wars. Let's take an absolutely futile example from the daily life.

DEMO

Once, on a mundane afternoon, a sudden mischief arose in my belly. Some song which played on the idiot box, gave me an idea. It was blaring on, about some association between the principal characters forever. That the lovers shall be in love forever and never separate. My brain started working. What may be the possible synonyms for the word- "forever"? Presto!!!!!!!!!! Internet, our formidable crony steps in and offers a million responses in a matter of seconds. Amongst others 'Amaranthine' was a word, which seemed extremely interesting, because, it possessed the three most attractive qualities a word can possess. It was (*or rather is*)-

Obscure

Impressive

Intimidating

Enough to give the mediocre language aficionados, few sleepless nights. Stage 1 complete.

Now what would be a fascinating partner for "amaranthine".

I wanted a synonym for the word-"association" or "alliance".

The word 'Concord' seemed like a dream.

Join the two and you get-

'Amaranthine Concord'

Beautiful!!!!!!!!!!!!!

The meaning comes out to be an eternal association or understanding or pact. Take it a notch higher in the realms of romance. The symbol of true love. Sanctity of marriage. The union of two souls for eternity- 'Amaranthine Concord'. So, with a little mischief and manipulation we have discovered a supposedly heavy and scary word which is all in all impressive.

I couldn't stop laughing at this travesty of a discovery of mine. Some may even sneer at calling this a discovery. But wait there is more to 'Amaranthine Concord'.

For the spiritual minds, it represents the association with the Holy forever. The unseen thread, which binds each and every living soul to the creator. However near or far they may wander, the Amaranthine Concord exists. Thus, everyone may perceive this set of two words, in their own way.

Every stimulation, is liable to multiple reactions. These reactions are subjective. They depend on person to person. We are all exemplifications of a signal receiver and transmitter rolled into one. Unlike, the man made device, we are not restricted to fixed transmissions. We receive everything around us. That reception is absorbed. Then it is blended into our psyche. The batter is kept on a flame of experience and memories including our losses and achievements, encompassing our blunders and simmered for a while. The congealed product is infused with our intellect. This infusion is now ready to be expressed or technically transmitted. Here, the retarding agents step in- fears, inhibitions, shyness, insecurities. These act like pasta strainers or sieves, which regulate as to how much we will express outside. That is the human way of thriving.

Raw knowledge goes in......................it is processed... ....comes out.................

A vicious cycle.

IV

IS MY BRAIN, MY ENEMY????

Man has always been a creature, who is highly susceptible to get bored. Boredom is something, which can rot the most superlative thinking faculty and reduce it to a dull and morose machine. Once, I had read somewhere that parrots can die of boredom. In the name of all that is Holy!!! I attest to the fact that we also are susceptible to this weakness. I believe, that even humans can die of boredom (*at least I can*). Though, it is not the death of the body, the cessation of heart beat and pulse, dilation and fixation of pupils or that kind of stuff. It is a figurative death.

Boredom can drive you wild. It has many levels and proceeds in a slow methodical fashion, step by step, each step coming in a paroxysm. It kills our brain. As our dear 'Sherlock Holmes' once said- "My *mind resents stagnation*". True as gospel.

The human brain is an exhausting ride. It has been built to work ceaselessly, forever. Whether we sit, work, drive, relax, eat, phase out, daydream, sleep or live in the illusion that we are resting ourselves, the Brain never rests. It needs an unlimited supply of raw material to burn. When we keep providing it with fodder, it lets us stay in peace. It has something to feed on, so it leaves us alone to pursue our objectives. But, when we are unable to provide to the monster, it turns nasty. If you do not give it raw material to burn, it will burn you. The brain has to be provided with things and fed with thoughts.

Thoughts to worry and deliberate about.

Thoughts to analyze and draw inferences from.

Thoughts to develop memories and take decisions.

Thoughts to create on and off switches.

Sometimes to create fear to stop us from doing things

Thoughts to appeal, to make us cautious and to give us experience.

Brain is like that ruthless Math teacher, who simply cannot resist solving problems and would not let the pupils a single period of leisure. Brain craves problems. Luckily enough, we live in a world where we are surmounted with unending problems. The brain has enough to feed on as the list is infinite and has a tendency to increase with geometric progression. Often, the brain needs to be provided with a sedative to slow it down (*but never stop*), to provide the man a moment of peace. But that we can and we do deal with. The more pressing problem is, when the higher centers of our brain demand raw material. These centers are those, which are not interested (*in fact are dismissive*) about the common superficial problems. Imagine the scenario that everyone has to go through, at many turns in life.

THE SCENARIO

We are reasonably settled. Work is going smoothly, no hitch in the personal life, finances are looking good, nothing to complain about, no pressing issues at hand. To be concise, there is no problem. Now we may act smug about such turn of events, but the juggernaut that occupies the penthouse of our body is not pleased. We have stopped providing it with woes and frustrations, which is its staple diet. It has not been designed to starve. It needs its nutrition and if not provided with, it bloody well knows how to get it.

If there is no problem, it will either create a problem or more commonly look into the memories to find a problem. It is absurdly easy to pick out an unresolved traumatic emotional issue from the vast sea of our memories. This issue will now be released from its cell and left to pounce upon us. This crime, is generally executed while we are sleeping, because we cannot forcibly stop our brain. We have been provided with an abort button by nature, to force our mind to turn some other way or suppress a memory. Unfortunately this button works only when we are conscious. So, during our sleep this villain (a.k.a. *our brain*) unearths a stinging problem, brings it to the fore, churns it and precipitates it into a burning issue. It already starts irking our sub conscious and we wake up with a heavy load over our head. Sue me if what I say is untrue and it has never happened to you.

How frequently has this happened? We have woken up with terrible anxiety and a nagging, prodding feeling of distraught over a long forgotten problem, or what was a laughably trivial issue at some point of time. Who has not experienced that terrible desperation and agony? We wonder, that until last night everything was swell. Thoughts like-

"How could I have forgotten about such a pressing issue?" OR

"I was so happy when I had forgotten about this" cross our mind.

Then we brood over the problem for the next few days. We are moody and depressed. We wonder- Is my own brain, my enemy??????

No. This is a common phenomenon experienced by everyone. The brain has simply, in absence of a thought process, discovered a new chain of thoughts to keep itself occupied. There is no malice behind it, nor is the brain our foe. It has been constructed to function in a particular way and it is doing just that. We just need to program ourselves and learn few techniques to keep it happy.

Man probably was never worth being bestowed with such an exceptional and advanced organ as brain. It is the most intricate, complex and the most complete machine imaginable. It is PERFECT. Harboring the brain is not a joke. It needs proper handling and maintenance. The brain is not something to be taken for granted. The only reason, that people have psychological and psychiatric illnesses or disorders is, that they do not possess the ability and strength; and fail to provide the correct environment for the brain to thrive.

The brain is not something which can be just kept and forgotten about. Ideally, God should have provided us with a set of instructions, "Dos and Donts" and an instruction manual on the proper application, care, maintenance and repair of the Brain. Sadly, we don't have those instructions. Going through the hell of the above mentioned phenomenon repeatedly, reading texts related to this from all over the Globe and talking to people, gives us some idea on how to control the brain. Yes. That is the answer. We have to control the brain.

We have to learn to become its master. We have to train it to follow, rather than to give orders.

Now, the brain is like a wild, free spirited horse. An untamed beast. Extremely powerful and useful but a hazard, which may lead to personal injury, unless it is put a leash on. If we learn to control the brain, to achieve equilibrium, it will provide us with its astonishing capabilities and inexplicable powers and intelligence. It shall unlock the previously inaccessible portals of wisdom, intuition and knowledge.

More than 90% of our brain is still unexplored. It is virgin territory, which possesses some of the most sought after secrets. In the hustle bustle of every day, we never try to penetrate the multi layered covers of our mind. We shall never need to venture out to seek answers, once we become the masters of our own faculties. The enlightened souls, the seekers, the hunters of Truth know this. They do not stumble upon the answers by making long voyages, arduous journeys or mountain treks. They achieve them, when they achieve the sense of being One. When, they truly understand the potential of their mind, the sacred entity which resides inside our temple (*there is a reason that part of the head is called temple*), the gateways to wisdom are opened for them. It is not a big mystery how it is done. Everyone knows it. At least theoretically.

GOLDEN PROCEDURE OR QUACK NOSTRUM?

Ok, now the following procedure may sound NUTS, but I actually tried it and was amazed. It will surely work for you as well. This is not meditation.

You want to control your mind? The first step is to calm yourself. Calming oneself completely. Relaxing every tissue of the body. Letting it loose. Disengaging and disowning the attachments and joints. Let yourself free. Deep breathing does help. Closing the eyes helps, because it shields the tempting exterior from our heart and lets it listen to us. It is not something, which can be done consciously or forcibly. The whole idea of relaxing is to release the force. The feeling, when we achieve it, is of complete detachment. We feel, as if we have left all connections from the body. We do not feel our parts. We feel like a floating lobule, located somewhere between our eyes. Between our eyes......this is very important. The funny thing is, we do not even feel that we have eyes. We lose the sensation of touch to the ground. After this, comes the phase when we start revolving. No body. We weightlessly revolve rhythmically. Fast, then slow, then fast. All this is not a delusion and can be actually experienced.

The sensation of revolving can be explained by a coherent scientific theory. When we are sitting down with our legs folded, the blood vessels of our legs get compressed. Then, when the body shifts slightly to re-perfuse the vessels, the blood gushes into them and its motion stimulates the peripheral tactile receptors, which give the illusion of revolution.

Regardless of its cause, the feeling provides immense peace and enjoyment. It is like being in a zero gravity chamber, but we are not topsy-turvy, we are stable yet weightless. It is extremely comfortable.

Now, we shall step into the stage of listening to our inner voice. To listen to God. To listen to the answers. Calm the superficial ramble which masks the true voice. All this, while the brain has been thinking frantically and we could hear voices of our own thoughts. Do not listen to this ramble. Tell it to shut up. Humming helps here. Hum to dampen the sounds. Hum to focus the energy between the eyes. Everything should be quiet except the humming. Your hum should be the only sound in the world.

Free of thoughts, emotions, feelings, worries. Concentrate yourself between your eyes, but do not force. It is a very fluid transition. Try to focus between your eyes, without wrinkling your brow. That is where the Third Eye resides. Clinically, it is referred to, as the Pineal gland. It appears to be vestigial (*not used anymore*), but we merely are unaware of the way to evoke it. Transferring the concentration between the eyes stimulates the third eye. It is not the eye which shall see anything. It shall unlock the divine in us. Initially it is difficult to focus between the eyes and may even cause a dragging sensation or headache. That is because we strain the brow muscles too much in an effort to achieve it. We have to remember that the brow muscles lie superficial. We do not have to exercise them. What we want to stimulate resides inside our head. Slowly and gently we have to attempt to shift our energies towards that focal point.

The centre of eyes is just a crude reference point. When we are successfully able to stimulate our third eye, we shall feel a movement inside our head, not on the surface. This movement is akin to unfolding or some fluid getting deposited at the base of the forehead. Slowly, we shall be able to do this anytime and it will become easier. Then, it shall become a part of the life and shall go on subconsciously. This practice endows us with peace, tranquility and courage. It makes us stable and unaffected by spurts of anger or other negative emotions. It is the first step toward achieving one's true self, the foundation stone. Progressing on this path, when we reach this milestone the method becomes self sustaining. From here on, we are not dependant on anyone's guidance; we don't need road maps or instructions on how to proceed further.

Back to the topic on hand

The objective of all this is to stabilize our brain. To steady our nerves. Paroxysms of extreme emotions, subverts a human beings balance whether it be joy, grief, anger. Joy, Grief and Anger are the Three Kings of the universe of emotions. When we respond to the emotions to their full merit, that is we become extremely happy (*when joy stimulates us*), or fly into a rage quickly (*when anger pokes us*) or go down in the dumps easily, it takes a lot of time and effort for the brain to return to its equilibrium. That is why, the wise people have always advised us to remain emotionless. They are not asking us to be any less of human. What they imply is, to be immune to the factors which may stimulate extreme emotions and destabilize the harmony. Meditating, concentrating one's energy and evaluating one's own self helps fortify this equilibrium. It makes us unwavering and resistant to the spikes of emotion. It helps us control our mind. If we give in to the weakness of the Three Kings, then we lose control over our mind. It is like losing the leash to a very spirited horse. Then the horse shall take us where it desires. The mind presents with hazardous and diabolical schemes and we meekly agree to them. In such a state we turn into a puppet. We have to be the masters, not be mastered.

The power to say NO. The insight to know when to stop. The courage to say no to temptation. The grit to act on our beliefs.

V

IS MY BRAIN, MY BUDDY????

Formative years of a child are a very nascent stage. Extremely impressionable. Memories start forming during this period. Strong memories, which remain till the dying day as if carved in stone. These memories are often forgotten, rarely remembered but they are a map to the journey of adulthood. Subconsciously, these memories stay and shape the particular individual. No memory is ever lost from inside a human brain in normal state. It maybe docketed, shelved, filed, compressed or pushed back, but each and every single memory is stored. The human brain is superior to the largest, widest and most extensive and advanced library in the world. It has multiple chambers, with multiple segments, with multiple racks and banisters, with millions of shelves, drawers and pigeon holes, each of which contain the record of a memory. Like any library, it is segregated into recent and ancient. Modern and old. Contemporary and history. Revision of all the dockets is done regularly and refilling and reassignment is scheduled. A new memory today, shall be pushed into the more interior ancient chambers until it is summoned repeatedly. The individual shall remember it foggily through the years, to forget it eventually.

The more superficial chambers are dedicated to the recent memories, fresher, glossier and precise. Some memories have the distinction of being fond or loved and are summoned by the individual when a cheerful mood is desirable, or in the event of some emotional consequence. These memories are repeatedly visited and enriched over the time by adding of wishful details.

Yes, the human brain has this phenomenal power of altering memories as per the individual's taste to make them more palatable. The sweet memories can be further sweetened and literally glamorized for a more satisfying experience during a re-visit. Industrial vocabulary may label this as refurbishing. Tiny specks of details might be thrown in for lifting up the experience. Unfortunately, the vice versa is also true.

The brain also possesses certain horrifying, terrorizing, agonizing and heartily embarrassing memories. The individual is never keen to summon them at will. These memories are stronger and etched deeper, compared to the happier ones. It is harder to forget these. They are summoned by the sub-conscious against will, at times of emotional vulnerability. Such times are-

Grief

    Fear

        Emotional crisis

          Guilt

           Anxiety

             Sleep and dreams

               Unconscious state

                 Hours of the dawn

Each one of us has been plagued by the most horrifying memories and thoughts at such hours. It is a part of the process. The process of building one's personality. An awareness of the evil is essential to develop a character. The pigeon, which closes its eyes on seeing a cat lives in a happy delusion, but is eventually eaten up. Closing our eyes to the worse makes us an easy prey, a soft target.

Good and evil go hand in hand. We should be aware of evil and respect it. It gives us a glimpse into the worst that could happen. Pushes us to prepare. Motivates us to be cautious, careful and take prophylactic measures. Makes us stout at heart and gives the courage to face the dreaded. To hope for the best and be prepared for the worst. Bad memories are a part of this Evil force in a big way. Whether we like it or not, we do visit and re-visit these memories again and again. They give us lessons for life. I have experienced it myself.

I was in a particular situation which resulted in a very ugly altercation. It disturbed me emotionally and I regretted the way in which I had reacted during the circumstances. It troubled me for some time and later supposedly was docketed as a certified bad memory. Years later, I found myself in a similar situation. By that time my mind must have visited the previous situation 100s of times, both consciously and sub-consciously. My regret also must have been duly noted. Now in the present state, when such circumstances reappeared suddenly, my mind acted automatically. This time, I behaved in a more acceptable manner, acceptable to me that is. It happened so suddenly that I did not have time to think, but my mind helped me. A plan of action had already been made and was executed before I could think. It was based on the previous experience and I acted on it at a spinal level.

My last bad memory protected me from adding a fresh bad memory or regret. In fact, it gave me a pleasant think to wonder about. Mysterious ways in which the mind works. So even if we hate them, bad memories and nightmares do serve their purpose.

VI

THE SOCIAL NETWORK………… REALLY????

In the past few years, in fact the decade, we have observed a literal explosion in the area of the Social Network. So colossal has been the industry, that it has made billionaires out of erudite professionals once shunned as nerds or geeks during the dorm age. The secret, of the success of this industry is, actually pretty predictable and primitive. The primal need of Man to stay in groups, for support and protection. Man is a social animal. We need family, peers, friends, acquaintances, lovers, exes, even enemies around us. Can't live with them, can't push them off the cliff :P :D. Jokes apart, our basic need to be near others of our kind, has now expanded to the virtual world. We like to be with each other. Man is happiest in company of his friends and family. Friends, even more than family. Families are our support system and we cannot survive without those but, there is a part of each individual which seeks like minded company. Company of people one chooses herself/himself. Like minded, similar aged, contemporaries with whom we can share the most intimate ideas, ideas we can't share with a blood relation. We feel the most relaxed and at peace with the world, when we are with our best friends. When, we are involved in lives which make us devote, an iceberg of our schedule in the cyber world; we have to find a way of satiating this primal need of ours, in the same world itself. We need to be with people, around people. Now when the computer has encapsulated us, in its amorous shell, how do we be with people? Even when we spend a major chunk of our schedules typing, tapping and jabbering away on our laptops, tablets and smartphones, that doesn't cause our natural instincts to fade away. We are not satisfied with a machine for company. This need of ours was reaching its frustration point, when BOOM..................... Abracadabra!!!!!!!!! The angels sang, the stork visited and our little, adorable Social Network was born.

The social network is successful for many reasons, but the most important, is the most basic one. It gives us the opportunity to be "*In Touch*", as many times as we want. Even if our busy schedules do not permit us, to meet our buddies, we are not far from them. The social network, feels like a warm conclave, of all the desirable people, easily accessible and near. Sometimes, we dread losing a person, if they move away, because we may not have time to jot down their new contact numbers or address. That fear is eliminated here. Wherever the person goes, they will always be on our network. People are excited to see the photographs, comments etc of the people they know. Familiarity adds to the charm and makes it more interesting. The biggest advantage of the social network is its ability to turn each and everyone into a "*Celebrity*". It is like a world, where everyone is under the glare of spotlight and their actions are noted. Each person has a circle in the network. The circle of friends and then the many circles of friends of friends.

Imagine, that I am speaking to you directly now. Only you, no one else. It is a private conversation amongst the two of us.

Whenever something significant happens in your life, you immediately have an urge to share it with friends. So, you put an update on your profile. This update is circulated around your circle and the many interconnected circles. When people react to such an update, the person who had put it experiences a feeling of pride, affection and joy. The feeling which comes, when your achievement is not only recognized, but is celebrated as well. You feel important and happy that your existence matters. Even if people do not react to it, at least they come to know about it. They become aware. You get a taste of the life of a celebrity in a miniature, yet satisfactory way. In real life, we would never be able to propagate any news so fast and so effectively. The social network, has also brought the world closer (*Once upon a time, they used to say this for the telephone*). Because everyone is using it now and is ON it now, the gap between people has become negligibly small.

The social network emerged as a blessing in our lives. It created the magical world virtually. Now, we are positively happy to be techno geeks, 12 hrs of the day and never miss on the fun because we have all our friends, acquaintances, associates and most importantly our "*Lover or Lovers*" with us, all the time. All are riding the same wave side by side. We are never alone, despite never leaving the cramped spaces we work from (*My apologies!!!!! This statement is not meant to hurt the sentiments of the more fortunate amongst us who work from not so cramped spaces* :P).

The social network is a wonderful thing, we all agree. Getting on the social bandwagon is an exhilarating feeling. The first time you sign up, is very much like first love. The excitement, butterflies in respective stomachs, the eagerness, the insatiable and repeated urges to check on your profile and the bliss and sorrow. It's the in thing, everyone is doing it. It is a statement, a way of life, a culture maybe even a religion to some. The bigger it gets the more complex it becomes. It is guided by unnamed rules, guidelines, cheat codes and punishments now. Though everyone is on the social network, few understand the game properly. It is just like the real world, in fact like school. It comprises of the popular kids, the known kids, the celeb kids and the unknowns.

VII

THE SOCIOBRATS-
"A MOCKUSCRIPT"

I really love this novel concept called- Mockumentaries. It is the lighter side of serious mass media. A take on something serious, but the take is full of fun and humor. You touch on the sensitive points but never offend anyone. It is often joked about on the social network, that soon universities might open, which would provide courses on how to play this game. Degrees and diplomas will be offered on one's excellence in this field. What if, all this came true? What would a course book of the curriculum for, suppose masters in social networking look like? How would it discuss types, classifications, features and give steps and directions? Students would study it and appear for exams at the end of each semester. Let's go through a passage from such a fictional book.

Chapter 3: Types of Sociobrats

Those who understand the psyche and direction of mob mentality, rule the social network, while others who ape the rulers or fool around, remain as wannabes. It's a cruel, dog-eat-dog world, which is ruthless in its dealings. Let's get into minute (*mynoot not minet*) details of this juggernaut. Details like the kind of players and the kind of games they play. Let's know a little more about the various kinds of Sociobrats.

The Leeches

The first kind, are those who are always online and "active". These people are self acclaimed celebrities, who believe that the sanity of their friends and the order of the world depends on their regular updates. They report about everything, from a nail break to an earthquake. These network leeches, never ever desert the network and are the most faithful and orthodox in this religion. When, they are your friends, the records of their activities alone, outnumber the records of the rest of your friends put together. They insist on uploading pictures of them in every mood, songs reflecting their every whim and fancy and jokes and anecdotes you neither care about nor want to read.

Ironically, most of these people are introverts in the real world and do not have many friends in flesh and blood. They may be the normal kinds, but are never flamboyant or rambunctious in person. In fact, this conclave of people was discovered after the advent of the network. When the social network exploded on to the scene, everyone signed up. Then, people observed a phenomenon. Certain quiet people, rarely heard of actually, were all over the place in the virtual world. They started being well known, courtesy their indefatigable pursuits on the network. These people enjoy the reflected light, like the moon and become underground celebs in their class, batch or group. They are frowned upon as being "Addicts" and "irritating" or sneered upon on the cooked up self importance. Regardless of all this, love them or hate them, the "Leeches" are the pulse of the network. The financiers and advertisers, who are pumping and gaining billions out of this industry, just love the leeches. If not for the leeches, business would not have been what it is. The leeches are those people, whose homepage is set on their favorite social networking site and being online is their way of life. These sociobrats have compulsive urges to post each and everything related and not related to them on the network. On a rare circumstance, when you log in and do not find a single post or photograph by a well known leech, you feel kind of rattled. It is unnatural and something doesn't feel right. The thing is that you miss the leech. You may tap your fingers in frustration, at the inevitable and repeatedly irritating posts by these leeches, but when they are not around, you do miss them.

The leeches are also not entirely useless. Generally, they are very large hearted people, who prove their benevolence. If ever you put up a post or a picture, these are the ones who are the first to like it or comment on it. They make it worth being online. They circle around the post, like a school of sharks who have the scent of fresh blood. Another thing is, because they put up so many posts and pictures, they don't care much about the number of likes or comments they have earned. It is so usual for them, that they are frankly bored. While with us, (*The Regulars; see the next passage*) frequently it becomes a question of self esteem and rarely life and death. So, a round of applause for the gallant but extremely misunderstood Sociobrats- "The Leeches".

The Regulars

The second kind of Sociobrats is the major part of the population. These are the multitude, who visit the network off and on. Never too rarely, nor too frequently. Their frequency spans 3-7 days give or take. These people, post pictures or comments occasionally and generally restrict their interests to their closest buddies. They are the good citizens, who go by the rules, keep their heads down and are never involved in anything crude, crass or ugly. They possess a sense of pride over their responsible use of the network and are particularly pleased that they are not "Addicted", like the leeches. They are also known to boast, that other peoples' reactions on their posts, comments or pictures do not matter to them at all. It seems, that they are above such frivolous vanities, but believe me, these are the ones who possess a dark side. They become obsessive and are known to check the network with frantic urgency, when they have posted something (*an activity which occurs occasionally*). The number of admirations or comments on a particular post of theirs becomes a question of prestige. In the absence of an appropriate public response, many egos and prides have been wounded terribly, leading to depressed and morose days of blue. The regulars are the nice people of the faith, who are neither too steadfast nor too tranquil. Despite the quiet and simple cyber lifestyle, the regulars occasionally enjoy bursts of popularity. These occasions are-

When they achieve something OR
When they go through an important life changing event OR
When they are going through a rough patch and put up the most controversial and brash posts

The advantage of being a regular is, that because your activity is not actually regular, every post you put attracts a higher frequency of reaction, than a post put by any other sociobrat would. You are not seen around much, so when you are actually seen around, everyone wants to know why you are being seen around. The cause for you to come out of the shell of secrecy causes a spike of interest amongst your peers. This is something that the leeches lack. They are so frequently seen on the dais, that no one cares what they speak, when they are on it. But, when a regular waddles on to the stage, people listen with bated breath. This is the reason for the spurts of popularity. When they post something, it gets noticed more than it deserves to be and the regulars savor their fifteen minutes of fame. So, if you are a regular do not fret, life is gooooooooooooood.

The Missing

We can very well understand and predict now, who "The Missing" are? These are the people who joined the network, just like others but are rarely or never seen on its horizon. No one knows when these people log in if they ever do. The purpose of their getting on to the bandwagon is an enigma. They are never seen and rarely heard of. They never ever post any photos, comments, opinions or even a monosyllable. They are there, but still not evidently there. They serve the sole purpose of adding to the ever bulging friend lists of the upper two classes. Amongst them also, they are categorized.

The Crocs

First kind of "The Missing" are those who occasionally sign in, accept requests, spy on their fellows, stalk their crushes, roam around the network with the luxury of anonymity and revel in pleasure. They never make their presence felt. They are like the silent crocodiles, which wade the backwaters in a shroud of invisibility. Their existence is merely remarked on by the fact, that they do keep appearing in fresh friendship notifications, which proves, they still have a pulse. These missing, are actually never missed. The social network is a different world altogether, nothing like the real world. The friendships, conversations, relationships that are forged in the virtual world are not generally continued in the real one. So, you may be great friends with a buddy of yours and might meet her/him thrice a week, but if she/he is one of "The Missing" Sociobrat on the network, you shall never miss her/him. If, on any rare event, a Missing sociobrat posts a photo or an update, she/he gets phenomenal response and attention. Her/his stock soars and breaks all records that day.

The Hibernators

The second kind of "The Missing" are those who have probably done a Houdini. They signed in, signed out, threw away the key and never bothered to look for it. They never, ever appear anywhere on the network except for the first day, when they join. They have a sparse friend list and probably multiple requests in waiting (*depending on their gender and physical attributes* ;)), which they missed because they never entered the arena, save the day of joining and probably once in a blue moon. The reason these Houdini's joined the network, beats me. Sometimes they create a profile unwillingly (*under peer pressure*), sometimes out of embarrassment on being mocked. But creating a profile is as far they get. After that, they never continue, because after all who shall bully them in the virtual world without their permission. A simple click on the sign out button and they are away from all the troubles the world (*virtual*) has to offer.

<u>*The Atheists*</u>

We also have to talk about the non believers. Though hard to believe there is, a substantial number of people, who still pull faces regarding the network and are not privy to join. The causes are multi factorial.

First is the group of honest people, to whom it really does not appeal. The grandeur of the phenomenon fails to charm, or even scrape the upper layers of skepticism in these people. It is not that they are malicious or jealous or have any negative thoughts. The thing is that they are simply not interested. The thought of being the part of the social community, is not something they look forward to. As it is, in the real world they have to put up with so many social obligations, why would they want to bear the same atrocities online? No thank you. They are happy browsing that part of the internet which does not talk back to them. It is a machine, let it be so.

Then, there are the types who may be called (*for the want of a delicate word*) Anti-socials. They won't do anything, anything at all which everyone else is doing. They will deliberately swim against the tide, ignore the popular and detest the 'Herd mentality'. Why should I join the network..................... everyone is on it. Anti socials are well recognized in the society. These are the ones who shall never attend your birthday party, never throw a party themselves and be particularly proud of the fact. These people are rebels at heart. They loathe the very social system and all its tentacles which surround us. Their behavior extends to the cyber diaspora as well. These people are not to be ignored. Many great personalities of their times have emerged from this sect of anti-socials.

Thirdly comes the sect of the Snobs. The snobs do not besmirch their "HS" names, by associating it with activities which the "common" or the "oh so LS" population is lapping up with great gusto. They do not step in the mire, lest there prim shoes get soiled. They only get involved in places which are 'exclusive' or 'by invitation only'. The snobs are those self declared superiors, who have an aversion to anything

'Common'. They do not enjoy contact, whether direct or virtual with too many people. They are used to moving around in a small circle, thus the social network does not hold any charm for them. These public domains are not for them. Some of them also have a class prejudice, so why would they enter a mad house belonging to the cattle class. The snobs are the most fascinating class of Sociobrats or rather NOT Sociobrats.

VIII

MY GAME, MY RULES

Working on the social network is not as plain as it seems. You just don't get on it and go with the flow. It is very much like the real world. You have to strive and play by the rules. Being successful is somewhat an ignored concept in the virtual world, but it is very much alive. When on the network, if you do the right things you shall be worshipped. The key is, to present yourself as a perfect concoction of mystery, glamour, exuberance, humor, and high headedness. Everyone is on the network, but few derive true pleasure out of it. Though, we start understanding the rules of the game after some time on it, we have to follow these rules. It is like you can drive a car, or you can drive the car in front, while everyone else trails you. When we are sociobrats, irrespective of the specie we belong to, we closely follow the activities of our peers. Some of the players in this game have alluring profiles. Whether true or not, they project an illusion of grandeur and success. They seem to be like the people, one wants to be. When someone does project such an image, she/he is a proficient player. You have to be careful and adopt a certain amount of tact when posting things online. Out of all the rules, The holy trinity is-

1. Content
2. Timing
3. Follow up

RULE I

People post comments, jokes, stories, satirical ideas, promotional messages day in and out. But the difference between a popular post and an unknown one is, content. We have to be sure that the post we put online is something which does not clash with our personality and the aura we possess in the real world. The best appreciated posts are the ones which are original. Do not be naïve enough to think that your peers shall not recognize a funny quote or saying, you have hijacked from the internet, or even an obscure book. Everything is known in this cyber age. When you put up a post by someone else, the number of hits shall not be as many as, if you put an original one. People always appreciate the effort one puts in deputing the gray matter to work and coming out with something unique and novel. The post which is put, should be an extension of one's personality. Suppose you are a well respected professional with a good education and a ring of professional colleagues. If you put up a vulgar or crass joke, it would be a goof. No matter how ludicrous it maybe, it shall never be appreciated for the simple reason that 'YOU' posted it. People expect something classy and erudite from you. It must not be a boring philosophical rant, but it should have substance and soul. If you intend to make your peers laugh, they shall expect some very smart humor from you. Go with your true self. Do not post for the sake of posting, or because it has been many days. What you put online, reflects what is going on in your life. People get a gist of your present mood. At the same time no one likes a bleater. If you are down in the dumps, or in a terrible mood, avoid putting anything online. Do not let the people know that you are sad and vulnerable. No one becomes a leader, by declaring to the world that they have been defeated. In fact at such times, the most happy and boisterous posts are advisable. Show it to them. Whomsoever has caused you pain, is very likely to be stalking you during such days on the network. If you show signs of a breakdown, that shall only flame their ego. On the other hand, if you present a picture that you are exploding with life, the world shall take a beating. That is the primary rule- "Always try to put happy and joyous posts".

I see nothing wrong or dandy about celebrating your big achievements online. If you do not tell people how well you are doing, how shall they know? If you have had a major breakthrough in your work or education, share it with everyone. Project a picture of success. The only caution is, to not over do it. Commemorating trivial events in one's life irritates people. If you post every single thing online (*Hey! Today I got a pizza for free, time to partyyyyy*), you shall only earn peoples' snorts and lose their undivided attention.

Post occasionally
> Post significantly
>> Post on the dot.

People shall lap up your achievements and you shall turn into a celebrity.

Your behavior on the network makes you what you are. Remember that celebrities have an air of exclusivity. They are not seen or heard all the time and everywhere. The rare appearances and the yearning to see them on these occasions, makes them stars. Learn from this kind of behavior. Manage yourself in such a way, that whatever you do carries weight. Be accessible and pleasant, but wear a shroud of mystery at the same time. Show a little and hide a little. Those people who put lots and lots of pictures, of every endeavour of theirs, are laughed at (*unless these people are girls*). No one is psyched about following your life through pictures of each and every moment. You lose respect and interest when you do that. On the other hand, if you have a bundle of few, but significant photos on your profile, each and every one of those is noticed separately and enjoys eminence.

RULE II

The second most important pillar for the social image is, timing. It is observed that at times, the best posts are ignored while the dullest receive a tremendous response from the peers. The time when you put up a certain picture or post, is the most crucial factor. I shall not shy away from the fact, that I withhold my posts and pictures, if I see that something more exciting is going on in my network of friends. Suppose someone has bigger news to tell people or a more awe inspiring photograph than mine, then it would be foolish and bad image management on my part to push my post as well. I very well know that my post shall never command the amount of attention that the rival (*or viral*), is commanding. It would be a waste to put it online. It shall be ignored. The response might not even be lukewarm. It shall hurt me in the long run. The time for its launch is not now, but it shall come soon.

There are dull periods on the network just like the real world. When nothing exciting is going on, even if something mildly exciting comes up the enthusiasm around it is amplified by a hundred times. Such a phase is the perfect opportunity to put your post online. It shall be like a fresh gust of breeze and everyone shall revel in it. Even a mundane post shall become popular at such a time. Now, this precaution is necessary but has to be applied judiciously. If what you have to post is something powerful and riveting you need not wait for too long. Just compare and analyze the present situation and if the present posts are even marginally weaker and you are a popular sociobrat, go ahead with it. If on the contrary, you have something stupid to say while some earth shattering posts are hogging the limelight, better to wait it out.

The exact time, at which you put up something online, is important too. Just login to see how many of your peers are actively online. If about 5-8% of your total friends (*provided your list contains of at least 200 people or more*) are active, it should be a good time. That means, this is the prime time and the chances of the visibility of your post are at a peak. Posting online when the attendance is poor will only cause under appreciation. By the time the prime time arrives, there is a risk of some other big story being popped up, which may take your sheen away. Once posted it cannot be reversed, so the post should be bull's eye.

RULE III

Another factor, which creates the image of a sociobrat on the network is their behavior. Each and every small nuance makes you the person you are. The friends you have, the interests you show, the pages you visit, your favorites, your taste in music, movies and other creative arts and the quality of your comments and posts. It is seen, that after a certain amount of time, people tend to react to a popular sociobrat's post, irrespective of its content. There shall be rigmarole of comments and likes on it, even if it is something relatively dull, repetitive or even irritating. On the contrary, something great posted by a lesser known commoner, might get ignored. This is the result of reputations and it happens only when you have spent some time online and have made a name for yourself, by using the above mentioned tactics.

Whether in the real or the cyber world, people have a herd mentality. They tend to be attracted toward crowds. When the numbers of reactions on a sociobrat's post swell up, everyone follows suit. Even if they had seen it immediately after it was posted, they react to it only after they see a considerable number of people doing that. Everyone likes to be seen in a celebrity's party. It makes them share the referred spotlight and gives them a false perception of fame. Likewise, when you are visible in a happening post, the chances of you being observed become multi fold. You would love to be a part of the festivities.

Another way to vanity is, to become blatantly classy. If you are popular, put up such a sophisticated or intricate post which goes over peoples' heads. Everyone shall notice it, but no one would dare to like it or comment on it, for the simple reason that they do not know the impact of such an action. Probably it is sarcasm and they may look like fools if they react to it. Such a post is so seductive and exclusive; that it rivets everyone's attention but has no takers. Dare to do this only if you are a celebrity in your circle.

MISC

Then there are other factors like how you have constructed your profile. Believe it or not, people scrutinize each other's profiles with extreme care. It is a reflection of your position in society, your success or absence of it and your image. It gives the person an idea regarding your tastes and preferences. People rejoice to discover, that a sociobrat they might be interested in, shares their enthusiasm in food, music, movies or sports. It also tells how classy or not so classy you are. If you are too much of a connoisseur, people are scared away as you project a snobbish and intimidating image.

RULES CAN GO TO HELL

Let's face the truth. The social network is mostly used to check out people, for the purpose of starting or taking a love affair forward. People stalk their crush's profile with ardor and may spend hours on every single visible post or picture. That helps them create a map of the person. It helps them form a strategy to invade the fortress. Pursuing a person and then charming them for romantic interests is a battle in itself. The social network now plays a huge role in this decade's love affairs. This is what happens.

You see someone you like; you trace them on the network. Then you teeter around their profile, struggling with yourself, on whether to approach them or not. If they know who you are and if you have spoken even a single word to them, you feel brave enough to approach them. The next 24 hours are spent in extreme restless tension.

If the request is accepted, the foundation stone has been laid. You go berserk with joy and everything seems beautiful. Do I need explain the twirling sensation, just below the navel each one of us has experienced in such a situation? The path ahead lays clear. Messages, chats, sweet exchanges, the first date and so on................................. until the break up of course.

However if the request is not accepted, well... .... you cannot expect to score every time. There are many more fish in the pond.

The human today has become so loveless, that she/he is rarely attached to anyone enough to break her/his heart. People are practical and I hate this way of life. Regardless, this is how it is. No one else, but the human is to be blamed for the deterioration in the arena of relationships. Do not blame the technology. It is a mere tool. It does not have a brain of its own (*Yet*). It does what it is made to do and initially every invention is done with the best intentions. Leave it to us, to discover the most crooked and disgraceful applications for anything new.

IX

RELATIONSHIPS 101

Relationships, the most complex and curiously enigmatic phenomenon of the mankind.

Humans............emotions...............feelings... ....relationships.

This is not a vicious circle. It is a maze with infinite passages, doors, traps, dead ends, alleys, turn arounds, dingy corners, bright corners and so on. The great maze of relationships. Human is born to feel, think, attract, get attracted, emote, love and hate. All these are the keys to the various doors, to access the turf of relationships. We feel, thus we relate, we relate thus we come close, we come close thus we find bliss and likewise get hurt. There exists only one rule for relationships, that being there is no rule. There have been the weirdest, most inexplicable circumstances on this planet of ours. Some scenarios so strange, that even the possessor of the most vivid imagination, would be hard pressed to imagine. These scenarios have either brought two people together or torn them apart. We can never postulate on a relationship. We cannot set guidelines as to the time spent together, physical proximity, geographical detachment, nature, appearances, stereotypes et al.

The worldly wise declarations of- *"This will work"*, *"This will never work"* don't affect the dynamics of a relationship. How often have we found ourselves gaping dumbfounded, on seeing the two least congruous human beings tied together? On the contrary, commiserating in dismay when those two who were designed for each other, not seeing eye to eye. It is unpredictable, surprising and awe inspiring how the human heart functions and executes. Every individual yearns for a spark, a trigger, a stimulus, a counter force from someone. This is something extremely sub conscious and involuntary.

When we like someone, we are never aware, that the thing which triggered that affection or attraction in us was something so subtle and innate. We attribute it to a number of factors eg. Looks (*further broken down into specifics like- eyes, skin, complexion, hair, gait, height, body and what not*), attitude, speech, voice (*that's right! Speech and voice are two different entities*), behavior etc.

All this is just superfluous and actually an illusion. What actually pulls us to a fellow human in that special way is much like a chemical reaction? We often ask- "If God really created two human beings for each other, why didn't She/He just let them meet without adding thousand and one obstacles, hurdles, twists, turns and run-ins in their paths. Why has God made our lives worthy to be penned as the screenplay to a Bollywood masala potboiler? A man and a woman (*or a man and man or woman and woman for that matter*), made for each other, two fragments of a soul. Legend says that in the whole wide universe, everything exists in pairs. Perfectly complimentary pieces, like that of a jigsaw puzzle (*only a 2 piece jigsaw*). The crests of one correspond to the troughs of the other or the cavitation of one to the elevation of other. Separated, they exist but do not achieve their purpose of existence.

Laws of Physics in Relationships

I as an individual am a certain charge (*take it as positive or negative*). Now, by the law of physics, I am bound to attract and be attracted to the opposite charge. Curiously, in nature there are not just two charges. There are millions and billions of charges disseminated all over the diaspora. These charges exist in pairs. As two of them are exactly complement, their attraction is the maximum. If they come in vicinity of each other, they should accelerate towards each other and get stuck (*speaking theoretically*). This doesn't mean that the charge is not capable of attracting, or getting attracted to any less similar charge. The two complement charges are made exclusively for each other, with their attraction being maximum. But in the absence of the mate, either is capable of joining with another charge which maybe the mate of some other one. The adhesion in such a case (*joining of two non complement charges*) shall be sub optimal. It shall not be as strong as in the perfect case, but still it shall hold.

Let's make all this technical riff-raff a little juicy. Something which is more palatable for humans who do not want to die of boredom understanding it. In this world there is only 1 special ONE for everyone, but sadly we may never meet that special one. Good news is, that we are never given the knowledge (*not in the usual circumstances at least*), as to who this single special one is. So, we never grudge or mourn the pain of never meeting that ONE, because we are blissfully ignorant of her/his presence. Though we never know, still the need to relate to someone makes us look around for a special One. Out of all the individuals present around us, we instinctively like the one who maybe the most similar to our real ONE. We are not aware as to the specifications of our true Love, but that knowledge is locked in the depth of our conscience and our heart uses it (*without us being aware*). So, in the absence of HER/HIM the heart deciding to keep us happy, chooses the next best. The one who resembles the original and makes us believe that She/He is the One. There is nothing wrong with this setup. In fact, it actually explains and provides answers to innumerable nagging doubts.

Why do people fall out of love?

Why does happily ever after never happen?

Why do I get attracted to someone else, when I feel I am in love with my partner?

Why does your partner lose their charm or attraction over time? (*This time may wary from minutes to 50 years*)

Simple explanation. Because we are with someone, who is actually not our other half. It is a very rare thing to find two people who are actually Soulmates and are together. Happens once in ages. Then why does this happen? Wouldn't it have been easier just to find that one and settle down. No struggle, no heart breaks, no pangs of love and simply 'happily ever after'. I don't think so. It would never have been 'happily ever after'. How would this world have run then? How it would have functioned? It would have been mundane and life would have terminated. Fusion and cross-fusion are the elements of life. If everyone's life would have been perfect, then there would be nothing to achieve. Nothing to strive for. Blatantly speaking there would be no spice in life. We treasure happiness, only when we fear losing it to the hands of sorrow. Happiness would cease being happy, if it would not be alternated with bouts of pain.

Imagine two people...
    Made for each other...................................
       Meet..
         Fall in love..............................
      Settle down...................................
     Everything is rosy...................................
  Lead their lives.......................................Die.

May sound great, but very difficult to bear. So what, if we are with a partner who may or may not be the ONE? Maybe we are the lucky ones (*personally I do not feel there is anything lucky about it*) to have been united with our true love aka Soulmate. What difference does it make? The person has given their whole life to us. Love her/him like they are your soulmate. Who is nature to dictate? Fight it. Make your partner your soulmate. Love so much that nothing else remains. Studied chemistry at school level right? Chemical reactions can change an element permanently. So change your partner (*if she/he needs that*) and turn them into your soulmate.

X

COMMITMENT PHOBIA

The most epidemic, rabid, well known, but shamefully concealed phenomenon in the world of relationships. Commitment Phobia is like a disease. A critically under diagnosed disease. It exhibits, what doctor's call the "iceberg phenomenon". Like in an iceberg only the top is visible, which is around 30%, while the 70% of the volume is hidden underneath the water level. Likewise, the people who are known to, or claim to have this phobia, or seek professional help for it are only 30% of the actual number who actually have it. People are scared of commitment all over the place. Some conceal it, others struggle with it, some fight it, some try to ignore it, but no one accepts it. Accepting the problem is the first step towards curing it. CP stems like any other phobia, from fear. The fear here is the fear of getting hurt. It may stem from multiple factors. A person is not interested in coming near another person, simply because she/he is scared. Scared of what you ask? Scared to get hurt. The whole operation goes like this. You are the "I" in the passage.

"I like this person. Probably she/he will like me as well? We shall come close to each other. I shall start developing a soft corner for her/him. I would become attached. We'll fall in love. Then I would get used to her/him. I would need to be together. When she/he goes away, I'll feel bad. I'll become dependent on someone

else for my happiness. I would cease to be strong and independent, emotionally. Then, what if she/he leaves me, cheats on me, goes away, gets hurt, dies...................... what would I do? The shock would tear me apart. I might never recover from the grief? I shall never be the same again. I would lose my spark. My work would get affected; my whole life would get affected. I may never hold up my head again, never enter into another relationship. I would be scarred for life. No. That is too much of a price to pay for intimacy. No thank you. I would prefer not to go close to this person. After all it's the 21st century. Who needs love? I at least do not need that special someone. I will not invite someone to stride into my life, wreck it and then waltz away."

This is how such a person feels.

Read the passage once more. Don't you notice a lot more of Is, MYs and MEs in there than SHEs or HEs and WEs. Let's count.

CONTESTANTS	SCORE
TEAM- I, ME and MY	20
TEAM- SHE/HE	3
TEAM- WE	2

Is this not suggestive? Is this not an egotist way of thinking? Selfish and self centered. This kind of thinking stems from the wish to remain happy unconditionally and perennially. The commitment phobia has its roots here. The will or the wish to remain happy forever, or rather the wish to escape from misery and grief. Commitment phobia is an escsapist phenomenon. We wish to escape from. To bypass all the gloom, which comes as a package deal with a relationship. The only way to escape that is to escape being in a relationship altogether. The voice goes something like this- No relationship, no heart break, no heart break, no tears. So we would rather stay away from the possibility of a nurturing element in our lives just for the fear of the despair we shall feel when that element is snatched away from us.

This does seem like a smart way, but even if I am strung up by my thumbs, I would never agree with it. I do not agree with those people who stay away from another human being emotionally because of the risk of hurting their own emotions. I am a strong believer of *"Better to have loved and lost than to never have loved at all"*. Loving another human being does not make us weak or vulnerable. In fact it makes us stronger. Foregoing a relationship for the fear of separation is like refusing to eat as we do not know which meal shall turn up poisonous. It is like denying ourselves, the greatest bequest of life. The greatest boon God bestowed upon human. Love. Fall in love and be in love. Love with passion. Love like there is no tomorrow. Even if we get to spend a single blissful moment in the company of a true loved one, it is far more meaningful than the decades spent alone.

What may happen if we do fall in love? We might lose our loved one. So what? At least the heart would have known the true essence of life. Maybe she/he was not the true soul mate, but at least she/he did pretend to be that for some time and did it well. Believe me when I say, the worst thing in life is to end up on one's death bed with the haunting thought of not having a single meaningful person in one's life. When we die our partner does make it worthwhile. Even if the partner is present or has passed on, the thought that she/he was there makes our existence valuable. A person who plays too safe and protects her/his heart from the usual pangs of love, regrets the most when she/he sits down to do the math of life.

Leave the self. Go ahead and give yourself up to another human being. The heart is not meant to be kept in a safe. It has to be exposed. The treasure of wisdom can be only acquired by paying for it in tears. The heart may be happy, bleed, get wounded, get ravaged or be broken; but none of these would be as traumatic as the pain of being lonely. Kick the phobia and try some commitment. It would make life beautiful, even if that beauty is two tea spoonfuls.

Do not end up to be that player, who had the best times of his life, but did not have a single person at home to cook him a meal. He was heard saying-

Sometimes I sit in my home for hours and keep staring at the roof, aching in agony. I wish that God take my life right now, but then I change my mind, because I am scared that there would be no one to cry on my body and it may be discovered after days.

XI

TYPES OF LOVERS-
"THE PRAYING MANTIS"

There is this one phenomenon that I have seen in relationships. This one trend I have had the pleasure of observing, studying, tolerating and experiencing as well. Ladies and gentlemen, may I present the phenomenon of 'The Praying Mantis'. This is a very strange phenomenon but so commonly observed and appreciated by people, that it is a wonder why it is not talked about more. The 'praying mantis' is just a metaphor I give to a certain element in a relationship. Let us delve into this study by the help of a saucy love story.

LOVE STORY

There is a couple, a quintessential one, that of a guy and a girl. Supposedly in love with each other. Supposedly, I say because now days the concept of true wholesome committed love is a long lost dinosaur. So, they are supposedly in love with each other. The age frame is youngish- anywhere 19 to 24, never more than that. This is the age at which, there is a false perception of having grown up or matured but a few years later we realize that there is still a lot more to learn. So a young couple seemingly in love with each other and surrounded by a group of common friends. Their relationship is the pride of the group and they are advertised as a symbol of love. Whenever the group goes out for movies or bowling or what not, these two love birds arrive together, leave together, hold hands at strategic intervals, share from a plate and coochie coo when the backs of their friends are apparently turned. They are the idol couple for many others and have openly declared their intentions to take it to the next step someday. The guy in the relationship will be called "The Wasp" henceforth for the ease of understanding.

Now, for some reason the blissfully sufficient love life of the couple shall come to an abrupt end. We shall create circumstances for the entry of a new guy in the girl's life. Is the new guy "The Praying Mantis"? Wait and watch.

The abrupt end comes, secondary to a change of scenery. The girl moves away to pursue something educational or shifts due to familial engagements. While a tearful parting the girl and "The Wasp" make several promises of life and death. A commitment to stay together and solemn oaths in the terms of 'forever together' or 'till death do us apart' are made.

The girl moves in to the new atmosphere and pines for her separated lover for a few days. Eventually she starts moving around in the town. A new character enters into her life. A handsome, smooth, suave, sexy and dead charming character. Behold ...."The Grasshopper". "The Grasshopper" is everything "The Wasp" never was. The girl who is already heartbroken and vulnerable is blown away by this novel chapter in her life. He is the ideal shoulder she needed, to cry upon.

The Grasshopper seems extremely interesting doesn't he? For more juicy details on "The Grasshopper" jump to the chapter- "TYPES OF LOVERS- "THE GRASSHOPPER", totally devoted to this rascal.

Now our girl is absolutely smitten and taken over. She just flows with the music initially. The human heart is a selfish beast. It cannot pine or grieve for someone who is lost, for very long. It needs a new face, a new thrill in life. So our girl's heart starts paving space in it's estate, for this new entrant. Initially she does feel the pangs of her previous love. The promises that were made echo in her mind, though very dimly this time. Then she gradually starts convincing herself to (*how may I put this delicately*)- throw him away. Initially she forcibly reminds herself of the innumerable times the "The Wasp" had been beastly to her, how he had made her cry, how she had sat up nights professing her love to him and he had coldly snubbed her. Now she only remembers his follies, none of his virtues.

Eventually she convinces herself that he ("The Wasp") is a guy after all and thus his power to commit is limited as per his species. Here she is pining for him, and there he already must have started looking at and checking out new girls. He would be making the most of this new found bachelorhood. All these thoughts start flowing like hot lava in the girl's head. This lava is actually useful; it helps pave the way for the new star into our girl's heart. She detaches herself completely from the "The Wasp" over time. She may have already declared to the world, when she was new that she is a committed girl. But that time she was not aware of the situations that will come up in the future.

She had done that (*if she did*) in throes of passion and unconditional love for her boyfriend (*Now ex-boyfriend*). This brings up a tad tricky situation in front of the girl. She has already broken up with the "The Wasp" in her heart, but how to announce to and convince the world of the new development, without losing her prestige. She does not want them to consider her as a ....let's say a girl with low moral values (*people call them by many dirty names, highly unjust because similar rules do not apply to guys; guys are called players, a very coveted title*).

So our princess has fallen in love again but is at her wit's end on how to go about it. Now she is very visibly getting distant from the "The Wasp". She does not have the same place for him in her heart she once had. That becomes evident to him also during their phone calls and text sessions. There are two possibilities now-

1. He has also found someone else and is speculating over how to break up with her.
2. He has not found anyone and stays faithful to her. (*Yeah right!!!!!!! *SARCASM**)

In both the cases they shall have a fight, not just one fight in fact but a series of rumbles. Both of them shall be aware that the end draws near and the fights are just the necessary pomp and show which precede any big show. They shall have arguments and shall put hollow demands to each other. Hollow because neither wants those demands fulfilled. They are just flimsy excuses to serve the ultimate objective. The girl shall stage these telephonic fights in present of the "The Grasshopper" and preferably as many people as possible to earn a sympathy vote. Also it does not hurt, that people around her are getting aware of a possible split in the future. This is the way by which she salvages herself from the situation. It is like-

'*See I was fully committed and loyal, but you saw for yourself how he treated me and ill used me. He suspects that I am cheating on him with "The Grasshopper"............*' BOOM.

If she says so we can very safely predict the future with the accuracy of a learned Seer. She has said everything in this one sentence (*ok two*).

1. She is about to break up with her boyfriend because he is not worth her.
2. The cause of break up is the "The Grasshopper" so the onus of her misfortune lies on him.
3. It is his moral duty to take care of her now, because it is indirectly his fault she is alone.

No one is a fool though. The game is as transparent as cellophane. People around are fully aware about, what is going on. All this is done, to salvage pride and self respect. When we indulge in such elaborate set ups for the people around us, the joke is actually on us. Honestly, people are not at all bothered about how we lead our lives. These hoaxes do not affect them, do not change their opinions about us and do nothing to disillusion them. Honestly we take all this trouble just to satisfy our conscience. We force ourselves to believe-

"It wasn't my fault.............................I did everything to save it..........................had to be done".

To be fair, everyone does that during the transition from one relationship to another. *Whatever makes you happy!!!!!!!!!!!!!!*

So, the final act has been staged and now it is common knowledge that our Cinderella has left her beau and is set to advance on to that charming rascal- "The Grasshopper". To be honest it was not entirely the girl's doing. "The Grasshopper" was playing his game from the beginning in a very subtle and irresistible way. He would in fact have been praying for the girl's break up. When she does break up, he has to play his toughest scene. Outwardly he shows that he is terribly disturbed by her break up, is extremely guilt ridden that he was the reason for her misfortune and vows that he shall do anything to get them back together. Inside the environment could not be different. His heart is detonating with joy, there are waves upon waves of bliss and it is Hallelujah! all the way. Like an early Christmas. He knows that the girl was scheming to tear away from the "The Wasp" since long and he was kind enough to give a push here and there when needed.

He could tell because he charmed her out of her wits and she gave in rapidly. There are tell tale signs that the girl is not too enthusiastic on being with someone else and she would not mind being with you. She never ever utters a word about her boyfriend. Even if the mention comes up, she closes the subject hastily. If she brings him up herself it shall never be in any positive sense, she will only trash him.

But again, at least the girls are honest and courageous enough to accept they are or were in a relationship once. I am one myself but I assure you- men are weasels. They would not even accept they were in such and such relationship with so and so. They shall lie, shamelessly and spectacularly on your face and be proud of it. This is part of masculine vanity- "to pride over lies".

The girl makes it obvious in a subtle way that- She is a likin.............. what she is a seein..................... (*apologies for the badly executed accent*). The break up happens. The world comes to know and now the girl and the "The Grasshopper" are the new item. They embark on the tempestuous voyage of violent love. Violent love???????????

Whenever two people come together after tearing apart old ties, their love is violent (*not in the physical sense*). They are aware of a degree of confrontation that has occured in the past. The pair of our Cinderella and "The Grasshopper" is a passionate pair. "The Grasshopper" obviously with his emotions in overdrive and the girl with her peckers high. The course never runs smooth and has major ups and downs all through. It could not be different from the serene, calm and cute relationship the girl shared with "The Wasp". This relationship is what potboilers are made of. It has passionate romance, over charged emotions, some scary action and a sprinkle of evil. The relationship seems on again, off again to outsiders but it is never off. The reason for such upheaval is that both the partners are strong minded and aggressive. The girl because she had the guts to break the heart of such an old flame to achieve someone new and dazzling. "The Grasshopper" because he never once shied away from helping her do so.

Now, for a relationship to work smoothly the partners have to be slight opposites of each other. It is best when aggressive pairs up with passive, so that the equilibrium may be maintained. That is not the case in this one. Both have the reputation of being loose fireworks and live that reputation up. Sooner or later the inevitable is reached. They break up. But their break up shall never be a calm, rational kind where the two hug and then separate, promising to be friends forever (*no one fulfills that promise but it is the standard protocol*).

The end of this love affair is an amplified and magnified reflection of its beginning. The break up is vicious, horrifying and blood curdling. The action in romance was nothing compared to now. The two shall have yelling sessions at workplace and in absolute public view. They shall not remain silent and harbor cold vibes. They shall have an open war with mass casualties. They never go out together again but make it a point to go when common friends are hanging out. This, so that they can have an ample opportunity, to punish and humiliate the other. These two are not the quiet types. Their friends shall be left visibly embarrassed by their outbursts but they shall not have a trace of shame. Then they shall have abuse sessions and issue threats to each other over the phone and text messages when they are away. Each shall not leave one opportunity to belittle the other.

You would be wondering, why I am turning this separation into such a blood soaked saga. The fact is I am merely relating the scenario in case of such a twisted love story. These are the mechanics of reaction which occur when such powerful entities come together and separate. The reasons of separation may be trivial to significant, but the fact is that two such high sources of energy can never stay in vicinity without bringing destruction. Look at the character sketches of the principal factors. The girl left her age old love for the "The Grasshopper" in hope of solace. She is absolutely not ready to look any further, but the circumstances have turned against her, so to a point her anger is justified. The "The Grasshopper" (*as discussed at length in his own chapter*) is an incurable romantic. Though this is the flimsiest excuse, it is enough for him. After all these mini earthquakes the girl sees that it is futile to proceed further on the matter and the two move away. Each has rebounds. The girl first and then the guy, but that is the end.

Ahan................I have a very smart audience. So you have guessed that it is time for the entrée of "The Praying Mantis". I have drilled you for so long with all these gymnastics of heart but not yet breathed a word about the character who gave the name to this chapter. It is indeed time to talk about the praying mantis. But you are wrong if you think the mantis appears now. No. "The Mantis" has already appeared in the first act of this story. Till now he has been, like one of the background actors in a movie who are in the credits but on one cares. It is time to bring him from the disgrace of being a nobody, to the honor of being the Hero.

XII

FINALLY, 'THE PRAYING MANTIS'

Remember how during her first love affair the girl and the "The Wasp" used to go around with a bunch of friends. Yes? The Praying Mantis is one of the guys of this group of friends. The "Mantis" has always been the gopher kind of character in the group, does not have much respect and is taken for granted. He is actually no one's friend but he tags along the group and they let him tag along. Poor "Mantis" is not even credited with the dignity of having feelings. So, he never asserts himself, goes with the flow and even tolerates jibes just for a simple reason. He is lonely and these friends are all he has.

Now half of you may have already predicted the earth shattering revelation I am about to make. The "Mantis" is madly, insanely, foolishly, secretly but unfortunately, in love with our Cinderella. Deep in his heart. Because no one considers him worth having any feelings or emotions, even if he is to blurt out some day, no one would notice. But here is the catch. There is only one person in the world apart from him, who knows about this. That person is the girl herself. Girls are way smarter than boys in these matters. They always know whatever is worth knowing. She knows he is M.I.F in love with her (*Madly Insanely Foolishly*). The "Mantis" has always nursed a soft spot for our Cinderella. When she jived into his life, albeit through friends of friends, he kissed his fortunes in pleasure. He has always treated her with extra delicacy and is averse to criticizing her even jokingly. The only time he stands up to a confrontation is, when he is defending her.

All this is very clear to the girl and she understands, sympathizes but does nothing else. When the 'apple of his eye' starts a relationship with a friend of his in the group he is devastated. Our poor "Mantis" is not someone who shall assert himself or fight for the girl. He has very low self esteem and cannot rely on his natural charms to turn the girl toward him. Any altercation with the "The Wasp" would be futile in his eyes as the girl would never choose him. Worse still, she might laugh at him for daring to think of such a plucky scenario. So he seals his feelings in the dark fortress of his heart and tamely tags along with the group for the sole consolation of being around his lady love. He derives joy in a shifting gaze of her that may fall on him, or the occasional polite smile or her smirk at a joke he might have told. The "Mantis" is far from satisfied with all this but he believes in the dictum of "something is better than nothing".

Time ploughs on and eventually the girl moves away. The "Mantis" pushes himself to express some of his feelings to her before she is gone, but is unable to. The girl anyways does not have time for anyone during those last few days except her lover. So she goes away without a proper good bye to him. The "Mantis" pines, but a small ray of hope keeps his path visible; at least now she is away from the "The Wasp"........................ too. When the girl reaches the new place, he is the first one to text her and ask for her new number. He stays in touch and the girl never minds him because he is so, so safe. Now the girl ascends on to her next multifarious journey. Obviously she does not keep the "Mantis" informed (*he is not a close friend in her eyes yet, just a pile on*), but he comes to know when he hears about the misfortune of "The Wasp". His heart rejoices in cruel ecstasy, as he feels this is his vengeance. The joy is short lived though as it is followed by a stab of annoyance. If she is not with him anymore, she must be with someone else and that someone else has to be a more formidable antagonist, because he defeated "The Wasp". The irony is that now he is left to speculate about a hundred and one horrible scenarios, because he does not have the luxury of being geographically close to the girl anymore. Earlier at least he knew what was going on. Now, she would never tell him and he would never know. Bitter, venomous thoughts pulse through his veins and he rants about in impotent rage. The only outcome is to wait, hope and pray. He has to sit out this one in the cold. He keeps in touch with the girl and exchanges pleasantries on occasions but conceals the storm raging inside him. The girl does remember him and occasionally finds solace in his kind demeanor.

Finally fate smiles on the "Mantis" once more. The girl has a violent and damaging break up with her high flying 2nd boyfriend. She is left scalded and bereft. She terribly needs a shoulder to cry on.....................again. The "Mantis" gets to know something is amiss (*girls are not exactly quiet about such things*) and his heart explodes in bliss. With the speed of a missile he fills up the void of the much needed shoulder. He is kind, attentive and caring. The girl is overwhelmed by his power to listen. Moreover, he never contradicts her or blames her. Whatever she says is gospel and whatever she did was God's pronouncement. This is what anyone sorely needs in such a time.

There are many who shall criticize you or blame you, but rarely someone who shall support you unquestionably. A person shall instinctively warm up to someone who offers nothing but soothing love to a broken heart. All the stars have now aligned and all points lined up in the favor of "The Praying Mantis". He is the balm to the girl's trauma and an ear to her voice. Most importantly he is something that "The

Wasp" and "The Grasshopper", never were. He is ordinary.
Yes............................ This is the single most important
point in his favor now. Cinderella has had two unsuccessful love
affairs with guys every girl yearns for- handsome, charming,
popular, successful, strapping, macho..............................
blah blah. Now she is disgusted by these adjectives. She has
understood the value of substance over sheen. She has had a
behind the scenes tour of a glitzy show and has come to face
the stark, ugly reality. Her brain is now revolted at the thought
of such Poster boys.

*When one's brain gets revolted to some thought it automatically
and sub consciously gets attracted to the inverse.*

Unknowingly the girl develops a fervent infatuation for
The "Mantis" (*"If you say 'The "Mantis"' one more time I shall
knock your teeth off"; is this what YOU are thinking??????*). His
simplicity, sincerity (*apparent sincerity*) and humble disposition
are a whole new experience. She falls in love with him, such
sincere, selfless love that she never knew before.

She reminds herself of the times, the ages throughout
which he has always been there for her, with her, rock solid. She
feels guilty on having treated him earlier in a cavalier fashion.
The days when people made fun of him and she used to join in
the activity. The days when, if she was at the receiving end of a
rebuke, he used to stand up as a shield for her. He has always
loved her, with such selfless love which never expects anything
in return. He never tried to enter in her life, get any closer than
he already was. He just waited and probably prayed. Suddenly
she has started seeing him in a new light, which makes him
look better. When she was busy looking around for true love,
it was always near her, waiting to be summoned. He loves her.
She gets reminded of the age old wisdom that is exclusively

for females. It is passed on from grandmothers to daughters to granddaughters as a part of legacy but is only seen in the fairer sex. That wisdom is-

'Choose that man who loves you, rather than the one you love'

Simple yet brilliant. Girls always love to be 'The Compromiser' in a relationship. That provides them with an edge in this power equation. *Do not roll up your eyes.* No matter how much love compassion and ardor is involved, every relationship is ultimately a small power tussle. It is better to understand the mechanics of this tussle, to avoid making mistakes.

Let us digress a little to talk about this funny yet plausible theory in relationships.

XIII

'THE COMPROMISER' AND 'THE COMPROMISEE'

The theory of The Compromiser and The Compromisee.

In each and every relationship in the world irrespective of the location, time and age group this holds true. Whenever two people come together, there is always an element of inequality. Inequality not in any other terms except, that in the eyes of the society. To put it bluntly- who is better amongst the two? How often have we commented on seeing a couple-

> *"She is way out of his league"*
> or
> *"I cannot believe how this guy is with that girl. What does she see in him?"*
> or the cruelest one
> *"He is better than her"*.

> You may swap the HEs with SHEs and
> vice versa as per your taste.

It happens everywhere. In schools, colleges, workplaces even marriages. You can see decked up aunties, snorting in contempt when the bride or the groom, strike them as insufficiently matched to the other. When a couple moves out, the society votes and one of the two wins. The vote depends on a host of factors- looks, career, educational qualifications, family background, wealth and success, though looks are the biggest deciding factor.

The partner who is voted as the better out of the two is called the "Compromiser" because; apparently She/He has compromised in life or settled for someone not worth her/him. The poor one who is the inferior of the two is the "Compromisee", someone for whom the compromise has been made (*no such word as 'Compromisee' in the English language................yet*). The Comrpomisee is supposed to have had a golden deal and managed to land a high flier.

Though this is an extremely cruel and disgusting phenomenon, it is very much there and turning a blind eye toward it only causes unrest. The couple may be passionately in love with each other and such doubts would never creep in their midst, but they cannot live clung to each other without contact with anyone from outside. When they move out in the society, people make it a point to make them 'aware' of the lack of equality in their relationship. They sow seeds doubts and leave you to water them and let them germinate. That is the reason we are talking about this phenomenon.

We do not have to let these seeds germinate and give off any roots or shoots. When we are aware of the true intent of the world we can go out prepared. We shall be ready and it would not be a shock when someone does actually start poisoning us. The World is wicked, it never rejoices at the fact of two people coming together in bliss. It always has the tendency to ruin relationships, cause suspicion and split two people apart. It is up to us to avoid this. Any and every relationship can work, provided the partners are ready to work on it.

Ok. Enough, with the messages and the speech. Now let us explore the funny side of this Theory. They say that women want to settle down with someone who loves them rather than the other way round. This is because they do not want to be the 'Compromisee'. The thing is that when you are a Compromisee in a relationship, you possess less of power, while the 'Compromiser' gets to call the shots. In a relationship the 'Compromiser' has the edge because, obviously She/he has compromised on you, so they have the right to steer the boat in their favor. The 'Compromisee' is in a slightly underdog like situation. She/he may be reminded off and on, that a favor has been done on her/him. So, the 'Compromisee' ought to be the docile one to keep the relationship working.

Now, when you settle down for someone who is madly in love with you, while you are visibly not so keen on them, you get an edge, automatically. Irrespective of the factors like looks, success, education etc. you become the 'Compromiser' at the very beginning of the relationship. You assert that it was not your idea originally, but you decided to fall in with it eventually. Even if your partner is way better than you in every sense, you shall win the power game and shall hold the keys. That is why, women pass on the Age old wisdom of- going for someone who is in love with you. If you do the inverse, you shall become the 'Compromisee', because after all you were the one who went behind the other.

Sounds ugly but it is all about power. The dynamics of a relationship are much more complex than anything else. It might be easier to rule the universe than working things out with your partner. That is the fun part. Even when you are two different human beings and you frequently feel like kicking each other, still you are madly in love and unable to live without each other. That is one of the most beautiful things about being human.

Caution: Please do not start speculating whether you are a 'Compromiser' or a 'Compromisee' in your relationship. No good can be gained out of it. Just believe in each other and love each other.

XIV

"FINALLY, THE PRAYING MANTIS............"CONTD.

So, Cinderella has made up her mind. She has chosen darling "Mantis". The talks get warmer and they express love for each other. The "Mantis's" emotions overflow and bounce like a river in torrential rainfall. He is unable to express his happiness, his relief and sadly his gratitude toward the girl. The one and only dream of his life has come true. They might have laughed at him, but it is he who has had the last laugh. He feels that after all, there IS justice in the world. After all these years, who could have imagined that it would be "Mantis" who would end up with our heroine. He was a dark horse no one bet on, but he emerged victorious.

There is a reason this character has been called "The Praying Mantis". He is a passive agent in this story. He has never gone ahead and intervened with his or others' lives. He just sat back and hoped and prayed. Finally he did get what he wanted (*or he presently thinks he wanted*). Though, this is a very common phenomenon that is being observed in relationships now days, choosing such an approach is not the best idea in life.

In this case, there are four major characters and the drama is set over a period of time with three major stages. The First innocent love affair, the second passionate affair with the charming Casanova and the final settlement with the "Praying Mantis". These characters may not necessarily be males. The vice versa of this story have also been observed. A guy who goes through two unsuccessful relationships in life, to finally end up with a simple girl who has been throwing him love struck and adoring gazes ever since he was a teenager. Whatever the reason, such entangled tales of relationships are the fodder for sensational news items. Human is the greatest conundrum and the relationships a human gets involved in are greater riddles. This being just one phenomenon, there are innumerable other ways in which people come together and then draw away, but the basis remains the same. There is nothing new on this Earth. Everything has already been seen and done. Our lives are a mere reflection of something, which might have occurred to someone, in exactly similar circumstances. That someone may be located a few miles away or on the other side of the globe. It might have happened yesterday or maybe centuries ago. The pattern is the same. Life does not have anything new to offer. This also explains the basis of life. We maybe different but all have the same origin and end. We are attached to each other by invisible yet powerful bonds. That is why our lives are mirrors of each other.

XV

TYPES OF LOVERS-
'THE GRASSHOPPER'

Now let's talk about the most interesting character in this sordid tale.

"The Grasshopper" though a charmer, is also a die-hard romantic and a Casanova. He takes pride in wearing his heart on his sleeve. He extends the same warm aura to every girl he comes across, which he extends to the heroine of our setup. He is not mean or malicious. He just does not realize that many girls have lost their sleeps initially and then their sanity due to his silver tongue. "The Grasshopper" represents the class of these hopeless romantics, who are actually a bit misunderstood. I know my clarification on their behalf would raise many eyebrows, but I want to share something, that I felt and observed.

This lover is the particular kind of lover, who sets out to find that one special partner for life and in his search ends up having multiple love affairs and multiple heartbreaks (*Pooh!!!!! Does that sound like almost everyone's story? Wait for more*). His intention is never to go around with many girls, nor does he have the deplorable habit of keeping a scrapbook of his conquests, like some people collect butterflies. He is never involved with more than one woman at one point of time.

He is actually a fool and a simpleton. He starts having fancies for whichever girl comes his way. He makes himself believe that she is the 'One' and goes Ga-Ga over her. He serenades her, spreads out like a rug on her path and showers her with love (*equal to presents in today's scenario*). Beyond her there is nothing in the world. He treats her like she was never treated in her life, ever before. Now, the girl is obviously blown away but ironically she is not the kind of person he is.

To be more elaborate, she is not his category of lover. She had been dicey about him since the beginning, but on his overwhelming display of love, she convinces herself for the time being, that she also is in love with him. She enjoys the warmth of his pseudo love. He is extremely expressive and that earns him brownie points. Usually men are not as expressive about their feelings as women, and they are left craving for that simple "I Love You" from his lips. This is where our guy scores. He showers, literally plasters the girl with sweet somethings so frequently that she is left gasping for breath.

This goes on for a while and the girl is quite happy and content. Now, the inexorable wheel of time turns over. One of the two realizes sub-consciously, that they are not actually in love with the other. Cruelly, it is always one of the two, never both together. It would be so much easier, if both realize that it is not actually true, but it is always one of the two. However much we force ourselves to believe about someone, our heart always tells us the truth. It is we who choose to ignore the warnings. So eventually the truth becomes evident. Generally it is our lover boy who realizes that something is not right. That is because he is too much of a romantic. He expects the girl to reciprocate his feelings in a manner which is even more exuberant than his own. He expects her to be as or more expressive than himself. That seldom happens. Females by nature, are more reserved and balanced. They do express their emotions but only when they are totally assured about someone and that may not happen for years. Then their way of expressing love may not be as loud and pompous like that of a guy. In this case primarily, the two of them are infatuated with each other but not actually in love with each other. So the girl finds it hard to profess her love for the guy. Even if she compels herself or tries very hard, she is unable to string those three formidable words together (*I..............* *Love..............You..............*).

In the beginning, the lover boy is patient and waits. But eventually his patience starts to wear out. He starts expressing his dissatisfaction toward her, initially through innocent hints and jokes and then bluntly. On a certain bad day, when he is already seeing red the cavalier attitude of the girl fuels the fire of his anger and he scalds her with a venomous outburst. After this he may apologize and the girl may pretend to forgive him, but relations become strained. Everything is downhill from here on. Gradually they start moving apart and cling together just for the sake of the old times. It is evident to the girl that the end is near, but our lover boy is habitual of living in such denial and is so blissfully assured that he refuses to foresee the possibility of a break up.

(The term" Boy" is being used merely as a rubber stamp, it does not depict any prejudice to age on part of the author)

SCENARIO 1

Finally one day it does happen and the boy is hit by its full ramifications. The incident which sparks it, is most commonly due to the lover boy only; contrary to what we may expect. One fine day, the girl is not able to tolerate his insinuations anymore and calls it quits. She knows about his passionate and overbearing nature. So she cuts him off totally because she is apprehensive that if he is given another chance to make conversation, she would not be able to resist his charms. This complete and total boycott hurts the boy like a kick in the gut (*I say gut but you are free to imagine any other more appropriate part of the body, which ironically rhymes with gut*). He is ravaged and devastated. He is not able to come to terms with reality for weeks. It hits him worse than the girl, because for him she was the 'One'. He had set out on this voyage with the understanding that it would be his last. He had given the girl the one and only place in his heart, worshipped her and fantasized doing thousand and one things with her. Sadly nothing shall ever happen now. The truth seems unacceptable. His faith has been lost. He sulks.

ALTERNATE SCENARIO

Unlike the above example, sometimes it is this lover boy of ours who is the one to break off the relationship. This event is rare though. He is too much of a romantic too be involved in ugly situations like separations. Occasionally though, the girl he fell for is so obviously wrong that even in his hypnotized state of mind he is able to realize the truth. Resultantly he says 'No'. Now the 'no' was the only obvious result for this match. If he would not have said it, she would definitely have said so eventually. But now that he said it before her, the girl goes ballistic. She had finally found the perfect guy. He had given her what girls crave for, in their partners- "Romance". He had painted her life like a larger than life, big budget romantic film which is shot on beautiful sets and in exquisite exotic locations. Even if she knew he was not the 'One'; she was perfectly happy and ready to make him the 'One'. All this does drive her nuts, but the thing that hits her worst is that our Lover boy never actually says 'No'.

He does not break up officially...............ever. As I mentioned earlier, he is too much of a romantic. So he cannot bear looking into those eyes and telling her that it is over. He is the ultimate escapist. He takes the seemingly kinder but cowardly way. He never says anything to her. He starts ignoring her and spends less time with her. On the pretext of being busy or sick or indisposed he reduces the time span of his interaction with her. The 400 text messages are gradually reduced to 50 (*give or take five*). Earlier he was the one to always initiate the conversation, now he merely replies to her. He avoids calls altogether. These are the warning signs. Gradually the girl starts feeling something amiss (*Dames have a 6th sense*). She rages and rants on him and funnily enough; it does not bother him now. He does not go out of the way to convince her and assure her, with his love. When she hangs up on him in anger, he does not call back.

The idea is that when such behavior will continue for days the girl will threaten to leave him. That way the blame of ending the relationship won't fall on him. This is again not malice, it is only selfish. He firmly believes in the Talisman "Breaking up is easy, breaking up and keeping your pride is difficult". So he does not break up at all. The guy does not want a burden on his soul. Tomorrow he may convince himself of his innocence when any guilt crops up. Slowly the girl understands his true motives. She does try hard to make it work. She knows he is kind hearted, so she threatens him initially. This does work for some time and he is coerced into speaking to her, but she feels a definite lack of warmth and adoration in his voice. Eventually her heart turns to flint and she gives up on him.

Until this point, we can clearly see that our prototypical lover boy though immature, impulsive and brash to some extent is sound at heart. It is just that even when his true self realizes that something cannot work out with someone, he has the super power to convince himself so forcefully that his very soul is confounded. Thus on a break-up it hurts with double the pain but also fades away quickly. The amount of pain that needs to be sustained is all borne in a short span of time. Eventually his heart goes into a self healing process. He promises to himself that from now on he won't search for the special 'One'. He shall sit back and wait for her to come into his life. He takes firm decisions (*Yeah right!!!!!!!!! *SARCASM*) and starts to put the pieces of his life together. That is one boon of being "The Grasshopper". You get over unsuccessful love affairs very quickly. It hardly takes you more than a week or two.

So our boy is up, set and ready to go again, of course with the firm belief that he won't get hurt this time as he shall let the higher power decide for him rather than taking things in his own hands. He feels that he has matured over this past relationship and has a better control over his emotions now (*Hahahahaha.............right*). There is one saying in the world which holds true in every era and place- "boys never grow up". When our new and "mature", fresh out of a relationship lover boy marches on ahead he has a resolution in mind. As soon as he sees a new drop dead gorgeous girl, his resolution goes down the toilet. He totally ignores that he had decided to take no active steps from now on and leave it to fate. His heart blossoms again and he starts devising plans to achieve proximity to the new flower. Again he convinces himself that she is the 'One', this time truly the 'One'. He has had experience now, he can identify. After all this is the age when you have to kiss many frogs in the process of finding your prince. He assures himself that this time he has hit the jackpot and if he does not act, he shall lose his soulmate. After all

God helps those who help themselves. These are some of the justifications he offers himself.

So the whole story repeats itself. The observation, the gazes of admiration. The approaching and the wooing. The first successful or unsuccessful chat. If successful the butterflies in the stomach and the sensation of new love. The initial text messages which make the bond stronger. Then the first phone call. The attempts to make the voice sound mature and husky. The frantic efforts to think of something funny and 'Cool' to say to her. The glowing pride when she laughs at his stupidest jokes or attempt to joke. You know what goes on. It is not that this new chapter completely washes away all the old memories. Many a times when our boy is in the state of self evaluation, the pangs of the lost love trouble him. He does feel a longing. But the new affair convinces him to please his heart. He becomes happy once again.

THE GRASSHOPEER has a weakness for 'Happy'. He cannot remain miserable, even if the circumstances demand thus. If happiness does not come looking for him (*it rarely does*) he goes looking for it. The new passage of love in his life blooms and blossoms. He celebrates the feeling. Obviously the new girl has some virtues which the previous one did not have. These virtues offer divine satisfaction to the "The Grasshopper" and further strengthen his belief that she is the 'One'. He blindly ignores the new vices which come with these virtues. Also ignores that her vices were the virtues of the poor previous girl. All this, just to remain happy.

XVI

ARE YOU GOOD AT FAKING IT????

No. This chapter is not about Orgasms.

The nature to embellish all the good things in your loved one while turning a blind eye towards the vices. Some would say it is foolish and naïve. But such a foolish person would always remain happy. When you see your loved one through these rose colored glasses you will always believe firmly that she is the most beautiful woman on the earth. You will never run out of excuses to love her, to fall in love with her again and again. You will keep her happy, and you shall stay happy.

THE THEORY OF FEIGNED IGNORANCE

This may sound a bit ignoble but is it not quite practical? This ignorance (feigned obviously) according to me is a wonderful emotion. You shall never see her ills because you refuse to see them. Such a person sleeps soundly at night. The level of satisfaction shall always remain high. It is nothing selfless or compassionate; it is in fact a little selfish. Generally it is seen that critics or perfectionists fail spectacularly in relationships. You cannot expect a living and talking person to fulfill all your expectations to the 'T'.

Your partner is not a book or a movie. They are a person with a heart and soul. They live, talk, breathe, feel and emote.

The malignant habit to apply your finesse to the person you love is disgraceful. I absolutely despise people who set up standards like a hurdle race or an exam curriculum for their partner or proposed partner. Should do this, should be able to do that, should look this way.............

Perfectionists generally end up ruining their relationships, because along with the expectations they have a delusion that they themselves are perfect and thus refuse to listen to criticism. They are immune. Please do not make that mistake. If you do; try to rectify it and control your behavior. Love your partner fully. Shower them with praises, consider them to be the best that you can have and the best that can be possible. The faults, as it is spring out from time to time. So try not to find faults. On the contrary try to ignore them. Obviously there are no rules in relationships, but this one does help a lot.

Now the skeptics would say that this is not the right way to go about things. They shall say that living in lies or living lies is harmful in the long run. I would only believe what they say when someone has actually practiced this in the long run and failed.

THE CROSS ARGUMENT

Though immensely satisfying, this system also has its faults. When you make believe that your partner is the best in the world you fall in love many more times than you usually would. In such a case, betrayal would hurt much worse. It would be intolerable, because you put your partner on a pedestal. Better to adopt this policy after you are totally sure or are married. I do not say that marriages never break apart or no one in matrimony betrays the other, but still it is safer. Another demerit of going moony over your partner is the collateral damage. You are Ga-Ga over your sweetheart, but is she/he too? She/he may not share the enthusiasm which you possess.

They may not be ready to overlook your faults or amplify your goods. The result is that you praise them or at least not criticize them, while they lash out at you, for your vices. This creates an imbalance of power. Due to your constant compliments she/he may develop a false sense of conceit. It may become so intense that she/he may start considering you not worth her/him. They shall criticize you and it would hurt, something like the blows you get without hitting back. Thus this card needs to be played extremely carefully and with tact.

Whether you like the term or not, relationships are all about the "Balance of Power". If you are planning to work on your relationship by this positive re-inforcement use a little bit of cunning. When you praise your partner uncontrollably you have to slip in an innocent hint or two regarding their shortcomings. Do not challenge them on those faults, don't even expect a response, in other words the mention should go off in the bat of an eyelid. Just insert it as a joke and it should be gone in a flash. This will please your partner but at the same time remind them that-

They are far from perfect
    You are perfectly aware of their faults
        You choose not to rag them for their faults
            You are sending a message that such behavior
                would be appreciated on their side also

This would serve as a nice conversation. Similarly about ignoring their faults? If something about them is irking you and you are being quiet about it, there are chances of a bitter confrontation. Because it keeps your nerves high strung, but you do not want to say anything lest you should hurt them. Don't do that. It is human tendency, that when we are not told off on our mistakes, we tend to repeat them and also lose respect for the partner. But this is not a classroom. Both of you are equals. If you tell her/him off, it will hurt them, if you don't you shall lose respect. The way out is to mention it without getting angry in the form of a joke. Let us take an example.

You are the guy and she has the habit of speaking loudly in the background when you are talking to someone on the phone. Say this and please do not be fake-

"I love you so much. You have made me such a better human being. Earlier when someone used to speak in the background when I was on a call I used to flip out. That way I hurt many people. But with you sweetheart, I don't even get angry!!!!!!!!"

Congratulations!!!! You said what you had to in a civil way, she got your point and she would take care if she has any self respect. (*Ladies this was just an example. Please do not feel I am prejudiced.*)

This way the relationship would remain civil. Like everything else in life, we have to work on our relationships, and the amount of that work is considerably more than in any other venture. If you keep on tolerating stuff tamely, the other person would never realize they are hurting you. How would they when you never said it. And you don't wanna say for the fear of hurting them. You shall keep accumulating the bile and explode one day. In the explosion, you shall say so many hurtful and unjust things and your partner shall feel terribly mistreated. Once such an episode occurs the relationships never go back to their normal state. It is always better to avoid such an inflammatory situation by venting out the steam in small and harmless amounts from time to time. Be nice, be good, be in love.

XVII

EXCUSE ME! WHERE CAN
I FIND HAPPY????

Happiness. Wise men say happiness is a state of mind. It is inside us, waiting to be summoned and to surmount us, to wash us over and to lift us. Lift us from the usual and routine, lift us from the state that we exist in. Yes, we do need lifting up. Because if we were happy than we wouldn't be looking for ways to be happy, craving for the mysterious key, the key that unlocks the portal of our most basic need- the need to be happy. But wise men say it is a state of mind and we should search for it inside us. I don't understand this concept.

Why if it is within me and within each one of us, do we have the constant urge to search for it outside? Doesn't this prove that we have been confounded? Do not materialistic things provide happiness? A new phone, a new car. Yes I have experienced it. These things do provide immense happiness. Those blissful moments of achievement, possession. We literally experience what myth claims heaven to be. So how come it is inside us? The car is a material. Not inside us. It is very much outside and a symbol of the meaningless things. Yes meaningless, or so what true wisdom claims. All these things are meaningless. They say if true self is achieved, if we open the portals of true conscious and inner wisdom. If we truly get in touch with ourselves or our soul, or the God that resides in each one, then we needn't pursue happiness. We needn't pursue peace. The man, or woman for that matter *(Pardon me I'm not a sexist; but ever thought- Why do they always refer us as only Man? We shall discuss this in "**Have we always been Sexists**"),* who achieves this may stay happy and content in a cave without any possessions.

Now I find this hogwash, and I'm sure so do many of my educated friends, modern friends, so called educated friends, friends living in the cyber era, friends who are using technology everyday to make lives better. I am sure we all find this hogwash. It doesn't come from within, how can it, we argue. We claim that it is just a propaganda for these supposed Godmen, who claim to be intermediaries, agents who can precipitate one's tete-a-tete with God. For what? To achieve our desires. Materialistic and wordly. Wealth, fame, success, progeny, love are some of the biggest share holders. But there are also darker and sinister desires. The desire to see the downfall of someone, the desire to see someone fall frame grace and lose wealth, fame and the worst life. You must have heard this saying being parroted a million times already so hear it *(or rather bear it)* one more time for my sake-

"Man does not grieve so much over his own misery as much he grieves over someone else's prosperity"

Simply put we are not worried about our own troubles so much, as we are worried about the lack of *(or supposed lack of)* troubles in someone else's life. This is the crux of the problem.

The problem of lack of happiness. This feeling of jealousy is an extremely toxic, slow poison. It has the power to destroy not only men, women or families but entire nations. It is a double edged sword. Like possessing an active time bomb glued to your body. It might destroy anything and everything around you and whoever comes near you but it will definitely not spare you. Your destruction is imminent at the end.

The basic need of human has never been food, shelter or clothes. It has always been happiness. Man does any and every thing to be happy. All the circus that has been pitched to perform, arose from the single basic need to be happy. Man wants to be happy. But how can we be when we don't know the way that leads to it? What do we do to be happy? Will wealth make me happy, or fame or love? And don't say it is a state of mind. How can it be? I never want to be sad and my mind is under my control, then why can't it remain in the state of perpetual happiness? Wrong. First flaw with this delusion is-

The mind is never under our control. It as an autonomous body. The mere fact that it resides in our body is not proof that it is under our control. We spoke about it in "Is my Brain, my Enemy".

So, if happiness is really a state of mind how can one achieve it? I do not believe in big words like- metamorphosis of the soul, transformation of the mind and body, striving for the universal good rather than own. We are common people. We are not Prophets. We have enough on our plates, without worrying for the welfare of the masses. Our wants are simple. We want to be happy, or know the secret to keep ourselves happy. And please no big words like- work for welfare of others and you shall experience happiness. When you do selfless service you shall be contended. These won't do for most of us. Let's face it, we are selfish. We are a part of the circus. Why criticize the circus we are part of. So what to do?

They say if you know the art of being happy you do not need any material comfort for it. The sight of a mere drop of water sliding down a pane of glass can make one happy. It is all in the brain or rather in the soul. Let us try to understand by the aid of a scenario.

SCENARIO

You were close friends with a certain somebody for a long period of time in the past. Busy schedules, work and social obligations prevent you from meeting each other and now it has been years since you even caught a glimpse of your buddy. Suddenly the long lost friend calls you and informs that, she/he is coming to your city for some reason and if you wish, the two of you can meet up. Bam!!!!!!! The first pang of happiness.

You are ecstatic (*if you are in the right frame of mind*) and enthusiastic like a 10 year old. It has been years and at a sub conscious level you have been craving to meet this buddy of yours.

You spend the next few days in an exceptionally good mood. You overlook peoples' faults, avoid getting into confrontations and pride over yourself for being such a happy fellow. Everything seems beautiful. The person has not even arrived. You have not had a rendezvous, yet. It is just hope and imagination. In the past you two would have shared many great and some horrible memories together.

Presently your mind is only remembering happy thoughts, fuelled by the blissful memories of the past and enriched with loving details. You choose to edit out the negative. That is the beauty of a happy soul. It creates happiness from happiness, positives from positive, it multiplies like rabbits. You are elated and your gaiety is infectious. It shall affect the mood of at least one person around you and a similar cycle shall start in that soul as well.

Now, as the time of your meeting draws nearer, your mind starts playing out imaginative possibilities of what might happen when you two finally meet up. It actually creates perfectly balanced, solid scenes in color and with dialogues, that too of hundreds of possibilities. These reels then play one by one or randomly in your mind and you enjoy multiple hours of blissful daydreams. You are happy and your happiness is swelling up like an army of ants around a sugar cube. It is filling your heart, your life and turning you into a better human being.

We believe that the cause of happiness is your friend. Is that right? No. The friend and her/his call is a mere trigger. The cause of happiness is the love and attachment in your heart. The yearning to be in the vicinity of their warmth once again. On getting wind of the possibility of such an arrangement, this happiness flows out unable to contain itself in its constricted container. It was always in you, but presented itself when you were able to summon it with the appropriate stimuli. The external factors seem to be responsible but actually have little to do with it.

Returning back to our story, the day of your re conciliation finally comes and you are literally bouncing on the balls of your feet. At the named hour you reach the place and look around. You spot your friend and rush toward her/him. She/he turns to look at you and her/his face breaks into a wide smile. You call out her/his name with a gush of longing and grab her/him into your arms. Another level of happiness. Should we analyze it?

The actual sight of the person and the power of touch, ignite such powerful emotions in you that it seems all the previous emotions you were experiencing were extremely subtle. When you saw the person and then embraced them your heart leapt in joy. You felt happy. Correct? That means this happiness was not inside you but induced from the external source.

Ummm.........wrong again.

Actually this is again spilling out of joy from inside your very soul. You did see the person but it is not the face that excites you. Your friend may or may not be the best looking person in the circumstances. There may be better looking faces around you. But they won't arouse similar emotions in you that your friend does. It was not the appearance of that particular face which summoned such strong emotions.

Then was it familiarity? Maybe the glee on seeing that familiar face after the passage of such a long time made you happy? Well, partly correct. Familiarity did play its role. Your friend would have aged over this time and the face might not be exactly the face that was etched into your memories. Still your eyes shall scour for familiar signs in her/his countenance to assure the heart that everything is alright. Though few changes may have occurred, due to the inevitable wreck that ageing does to a person, or due to the fight the person puts to avoid this inevitable wreck (*Botox, Fillers, Venom pack*), still behind this probably new face is the same person who was once a close associate. Familiarity is not exactly what has incited this happiness in you.

Then what is the thing exactly? It is again (*sorry for the boring answer again and again*) Love.

Your love for the person (platonic in this case) was already lighting up your days following up to the actual rendezvous. You remember that it was overflowing. Now when the heart is made aware of the actual presence of your loved one near you, it starts gushing and spouting this emotion. The joy literally lifts you up in the air. It rises in a crescendo which has no peak. It merely knows how to keep on swelling and swelling more. It does not know what to do with itself. Of all the experiences and emotions, only happiness is one which is infinite. Happiness has no boundaries and it is never enough. That is why it is the most sought after feeling in the world. The joy of seeing your buddy swells up the already overflowing heart and fills you with happiness. It makes you giddy and light headed. Welcome you have experienced the most powerful intoxicant or narcotic of all time, Happiness. So, again the trigger for this immeasurable happiness may have been external but origin was from deep within. It has nothing exotic about it and it was not definitely pumped into you with a tube. It arose in waves from within the soul and washed away your whole persona.

XVIII

YOU'RE HONOR, I OBJECT!!!!!!

Fine. You may say- "this is one point of view." I have somewhat proven my theory and explained it through. But now we come to the difficult part. The skeptics will be harder to convince now. The next step in your meeting was to embrace your friend. Remember we left you at the point where you two were hugging each other. Now we all know that hugging someone (*provided that this someone is someone desirable and the hug is consensual*) gives us immense support, joy and unimaginable happiness. When you hugged your friend, you experienced something ethereal that you never experienced all these days, merely thinking about her/him. It gave you joy. Now how does something like that come from within? It is definitely external. How does it explain the theory that happiness is a state of mind?

This is how I see it. You called out your friends name and fell into their arms. Let us give some names to the characters to make the process easier. Let's say your friend's name is Alex (*can be the name of a guy or a girl; yes I am sly* ;-) :-P).

So you see Alex, rush toward her/him, shout out- "Alex!!!!" and hug her/him.............................. and you feel very happy. Then what? 5..........10..........15........................ maximum 30 seconds later you break apart. You do not remain stuck to Alex do you? You leave her/him. But you are still happy. The breaking of the hug did not break the chain of happiness. Though you two broke apart and are now probably sitting at opposite ends of a table, you are still happy. Get the gist?

Alex was not the source of happiness. She/he was the trigger. If Alex would have been the cause and effect you would not have left her/him. It is not the intimacy of your bodies which gave you joy. It is not the proximity. Neither the feeling of hearing her/his heart beat against yours nor the fragrance of her/his perfume or the lack of it. If that would have been the case you would not have left Alex and neither would have she/he. Or the moment you drove away that glow of joy would have extinguished, but it did not. You were still happy when you broke apart. You are still happy now. Happy and content.

The source of the happiness is again your heart. It is just that the stimulus has grown stronger over the period of time. Initially it was just the Thought, then it was the Sight and lastly it was Touch. The strength of the stimulus amplified and so did the burst of happiness from the heart.

On hugging you had a literal explosion of joy, joy that was inside your heart and which surged through every fiber of your body. The feeling of elation is homologous, innate, that is it has nothing to do from outside. Neither Alex, nor the place, nor the environment (*or the way they say- "ambience"*) have got anything to do with your happiness in any way, other than being the stimuli and the triggers.

Happiness IS inside our soul. It is always there, though the difficulty is that it is locked and inaccessible. Extremely powerful and positive thoughts are required to unlock happiness. Not everyone, in fact very precious few of us are capable of enabling themselves, to summon such powerful vibrations inside the heart, so as to unlock the portal of happiness and attain joy. Yes, this is true. We can achieve infinite and perpetual happiness without the need for external triggers once we reach such a level. From what I have seen, heard and read, reaching that pedestal is extremely arduous. It requires tremendous amount of focus, concentration, will power, control over desires, reigning in of senses and stuff like that. That's why for the common people like us, happiness lies in external and materialistic things. We are unable in a normal state, to condition ourselves to beckon such powerful stimuli in our heart itself which can make us happy. Thus we depend on external things- a new car, a sophisticated smartphone, meeting an old friend, travelling to a new place, festive occasions and such.

Though we may not be so powerful, sub consciously we actually do practice the exercise of making ourselves happy. Without knowing, each one of us has stumbled on to the treasure of happiness inside our souls many times in our lives.

Day Dreams

Have you not ever day dreamed. Day dreams are perfect examples of creating illusions, strong almost real illusions which act as triggers to happiness. When we day dream we collect and execute the most desirable situations in our mind. Everything goes our way, unlike in the real world. We always emerge from our daydreams with the utmost bliss and satisfaction. This is proof that we are capable of making ourselves happy any time, any moment and it is under our control. If you feel happy going to a particular place and it leaves you content, it is not about the place. The key to a particular happiness is connected to that particular place and it opens up the lock when you reach that place. That place weighs down on that bit of joy but is not indispensible. It is all inside us, waiting to be summoned. We just need to take things in control.

Now few of my friends may still be skeptical (*let's face it, they shall remain skeptical even when they read the whole passage and no matter how many statements I make to support my theory. Actually this is one thing about human nature I love; the undying zest for perfection* ☺).

Man has to suffer innumerable hardships, has to struggle for everything in life. Our brains are buzzing with so many things to worry about and stress is taking toll. How in such a scenario, can we summon powerful memories to make or keep ourselves happy. That exactly, my friend is the reason this is difficult. Happiness is not something which comes cheap. If it was so easy to attain it, it would not have been so coveted (*another reflection of human nature, as soon as something becomes easily available it also becomes less desirable; we are by default attracted to things which are-"hard to get"*).

If happiness was so easy to find or summon there would have been no need for this treasure hunt. The world is a web of commitments, boundations and occupations. We have been burdened with such a multitude of tasks and duties that the time is always less than the chores. It is a constant race against time and the plan is to keep us so occupied in the less important things that we are never able to sit back and think about the greater good. The key is to seek the path to enlightenment while staying entangled in this mesh and performing all the chores.

It is like the juggler who is balancing so many balls that only two are in his hands while the rest are in the air. We are those jugglers who do not have a single ball in our hands, all are in the air. By enlightenment, I definitely do not mean to become a yogi, leave the world and walk off to the mountains or a jungle for inner peace. That is stupid and in fact cowardly. The challenge is to achieve the state while still fulfilling our duties of the ground. It must be easy to go on to the path of realization by letting go off of the family and shirking all the duties. Blatant escapism is what I think it is. Stay here, face the world and then achieve it.

XIX

NEGATIVE HAPPINESS?
THEORY OF ADSORPTION

We are back to square one. Did we get anything out of all this discussion?

Yes we did. Believe me when I say that we were not beating around the bush or the pond for that matter. We got to know a few things. The key to happiness lies inside us. We can keep ourselves happy or strive to do that, or at least pull ourselves out of a grieving state by conditioning our mind. Also this is easier said than done as the material world has kept us stuck in its clutches and such powerful motivation is hard to achieve. So the question remains; what to do? Actually I fear precious few people may know or pretend to know the answer to this problem. We can do the best with what we know.

I believe that an equilibriated state of mind and heart can guide us to happiness.

First few pre-requisites. One's happiness should never come at the cost of someone else's sorrow. Sadistic pleasure is sin. Now don't roll your eyes. It is sin. Why? Let us discuss why should we not do this. It is devilish, a bad thing, not a humane thing to do. *Do I hear a snort?*

Yes, I know this reason would not deter most of us from doing it. All this humanity mumbo jumbo is boring and nothing else. So let us come to some cast iron reasons.

If we derive happiness by troubling someone else that joy is impure. It is contaminated by someone else's sorrow and is not complete or fulfilling. It is negative and eventually destructive. It is short lived and agonizing in the end. It is not true happiness in essence, might be fun but never happiness. Even if we are a tad heartless and able to extract joy out of watching someone suffer it would not add anything. It would not be like the happiness which causes the soul to blossom and makes existence worthwhile. It would be a savage, negative lust like emotion which would only cause the deterioration of our soul. And it depicts the phenomenon of rebound. Popularly called- payback, making scores even or vengeance.

Whether we believe it or not, a moment of joy derived out of someone else's agony always follows up with a life time of grief. That is God's way of settling scores. There is no set time frame and it may take minutes to ages, but it always does, and the longer it takes to come the harder it is. It always reminds us of our deeds (*though we may choose to become temporarily amnesic*) and we know exactly why we are being punished. This reason is valid enough, is it not? So please try not to find your own happiness in others' sorrows, because it shall hurt real bad, sometime later.

We are going to be happy but we want a simple path and we definitely want no negatives. This is how far we have reached. Congratulations.

We have already laid the first foundation stone. The moment we decide not to bother others we are already set to gain some divine happiness. Now the next step?

For God's sake please don't say- "Meditate". Do not say meditate, look into your soul or blah…………..blah…………. chuck these big things.

The simple way to be happy is exactly that- *"Be Simple"*. By simple I do not mean wearing simple clothes, sleeping on a straw mat and eating gruel. Simple means to extract happiness from everyday things. Small things, little things, minute things. There are millions of occasions to be happy in any average individual's day. Small moments can be filled with bursts of joy. Little things can be turned into excuses to smile. Routine talks can be twisted into jokes to invent a reason to laugh. Every single day offers so many chances to be happy, so infinitely happy that the jaws would start hurting. The problem is that we overlook these because we are greedy for spectacular occasions to be happy. The big occasions will make you as happy as these small ones. Do not use calculation where happiness is concerned. It is nothing about quantity and everything about quality. Happiness is not measured, never quantitated. It is experienced and enjoyed.

You wake up, get ready, go to work. When you are walking down to the place you sit, you pass 'n' number of people. It is the same walk everyday. You work, have lunch, work some more, return home, watch TV, have dinner, go off to sleep. Mundane. No joy. infuse it with happiness.

Crack jokes, recollect funny stories, if you do not have funny stories, cook them up. Laugh exuberantly at others' stupidest jokes. It is no crime stealing a funny incident that happened to someone and sharing it as your own. Do a good turn to someone without any reason. Help someone in dire need of help and then demand them to say thank you. Listen to your heart. The heart is the Master of happiness. The only caution that is to be taken is that if it is given too much free hand it may go haywire. It has to be kept under control. But once you are sure you are in charge, listen to it.

The heart is a pure and honest fellow. Heart never schemes or designs against others. It does not derive pleasure the negative way. Heart only revels in untainted, chaste happiness. Over ages we have been strictly warned against the perils of following what our heart says. We have been conditioned such that the voice of the heart is now synonymous with, "Voice of EVIL". We believe that heart forever leads us to the wrong way. This is not true. The heart is a mere reflection or mouth piece of the soul and soul is forever pure. Even the skeptics would agree with me on the purity of the soul. Soul is not evil or malicious. It is a fragment of God. The human being is like charcoal not a sponge. There is a difference between the two. A sponge absorbs (*with a 'B'*) while the charcoal adsorbs (*with a 'D'*). We aDsorb. To understand this better, let us take a brief elementary science class.

Adsorption is the phenomenon or activity displayed
by substances like charcoal in which, when it is kept in the
environment, the surrounding particles come and get stuck to its
surface. The surface not the interior. The particulate which cling
to the surface of charcoal do not change its properties or nature.
They are just stuck to its surface. This is called Adsorption.

The human being is a similar entity. We are pure in form and essence. The time we are born our body or mind is just an ornament of the soul. The soul speaks to us through the heart. Over time when we are exposed to the polluted environment of the world (*I hope we understand that pollution here does not refer to that caused by smoke from vehicles and factories*), we start adsorbing undesirable and noxious elements on to the soul. It gets covered or rather coated with grime.

This grime is formed of everything exotic (*Exotic is not always a good thing*) to a basic human nature. The seemingly nice things are the material pleasures while the unpleasant are vices like- anger, jealousy, avarice, insecurity, grief etc.

Thus whatever actions we commit are performed by us, but motivated by these adsorbed elements. When we do something evil or inhuman it is not something that our heart told us to do. Do not blame it on the heart. It was performed by us, misguided by the plethora of devilish elements which are stuck to our soul now. We ignore the voice of our conscious, which is the voice of our heart, who is the spokesperson of our soul.

Do you know what this means? We are all alike. No one is born good or bad. It is only the power of an individual to make herself/himself good or bad. We can ignore our inner voices or force ourselves to listen to and abide by them. We may give in to the temptation of following the wrong way or we may choose the righteous. We always have a choice. That is the only permanent thing. Choice. Now what has all this got to do with happiness? Sorry I have a habit to digress. The meaning of this digression was to exonerate the poor heart.

Heart has hereby been cleared of all charges. Listening to the heart does not lead us to the wrong path. What needs to be done is to listen to the true voice of heart. Singling out the true voice out of cacophony of noises inside us. Quieten the undesirable voices and listen to the one true voice. When we are able to do that we shall have the correct answer to every problem, and we all know what happens when we have the correct answer. We feel happy. We just have to sandpaper away the pollutants which are adsorbed to the surface of our soul. A complete scrubbing is not required. Just a small spot will do from which we shall be able to hear the true voice. *Too many metaphors right?*

Practically what we have to do is this. A situation crops up. We have to decide what would be best to do. Now according to the type of individual one is a decision shall be formed. Please re-assess this decision. Weigh it and try to play out the possible scenarios in your head. Whether we choose to ignore it or not, God has given us power to distinguish between right and wrong. We always know that what we are about to do is right or wrong. If the decision we have taken and are about to execute stands out as a sore note, chuck it. It is not right. You do understand what I say. Just a little bit of courage is needed to act on it. So do listen to your heart. Untainted and innocent heart. It shall always guide you to happiness. Such happiness which is ethereal and mystic. Which shall fill you up and turn you into a source of happiness. You shall become a generator and transmitter of happiness. This is that kind of happiness which keeps a person content in a cave.

Happiness derived from a new car, a new beachside villa or a diamond studded time piece is undoubtedly happiness too. But it does not fill you up. It is short lived and attracts a lot of negative vibes from the world. It becomes injured by the ill feelings of the society. It does not remain complete. It is something which can be taken away from us as it has been derived by the satiation of materialistic needs. It has been generated by the pollutants stuck to or adsorbed on our soul. That is why it does give us a momentary spike of joy but not that essence of fulfillment. It does nothing to make our soul happy. The soul yearns for joy which satisfies its innate needs. Which is pure and everlasting. Which cannot be snatched away from it. And which does not attract the negative vibes of the world. Which keeps it in a state of lucidity. It may be derived from simple and small things.

Travelling, taking pains.

Searching the florists of the entire city to find a stem of that rare flower your sweetheart loves, and then rushing to her/him to keep it on her/his bed side so that she/he opens her/his eyes to behold it.

The sensation you experience when you see her/his face is true, pure soulful happiness. Soulful happiness is the happiness of giving. When you give something only with the sole objective of making someone unbelievably happy you get a lot in return. The happiness derived from a selfless act of kindness is pure soulful happiness. It stays in us like the fragrance of incense sticks stays in a closed room. The power of giving is the most underestimated power in the world. Probably because people are not worth giving anymore. When you do something for someone selflessly, when you do give without any expectation in return, you at least expect not to be fooled. When that happens, people lose faith in the power of giving. They refuse to believe in the concept anymore. It happens a lot. It has happened a lot to me too. When you gave everything you could summon and everything you had to labor for, when you gave your heart and soul to someone and in return they crushed you and disposed you off, like a used straw (*or used anything for that matter*). I understand the feeling. Such a stab makes you lose faith, lose faith in happiness, in good deeds, in God, in humanity, in love. But that is the test of endurance.

I am not saying that, meekly go and get fooled by someone else. The only thing to do is, to enrich your mind with this valuable new experience, but to never let go on the faith. Never give up. Follow your heart.

XX

HEART: *"WHY DO YOU ALWAYS BLAME IT ON ME?"*

Follow your heart. It shall take you to deliverance.

Really? Is heart capable of doing that? Can the heart be trusted?

The heart seeks happiness, feeds on happiness. The purpose of heart is not to be successful, achieving a livelihood or excelling in a materialistic pursuit. Its purpose is the most fundamental need of a living element. Peace. Peace is something which is not to be confused with happiness. Peace is a state which is rarely achieved in the present day pandemonium. Peace is not something which can be achieved merely by going to a desolate place, or closing one's eyes in mock meditation, or reducing the level of one's physical activity. Peace has nothing to do with exterior or environment. It is something very innate. You may be at the most serene, scenic spot in the world with all the calm and quiet that may be desirable, but there might be a storm raging inside you. As, it can be very rightly said- peace is a state of mind.

Mind or heart? Shouldn't it be a state of heart? We attach a lot of importance to this discrimination between mind and heart. Are these two entities really so dissimilar in a human being? Wise old men, our ancestors have always stressed the need to listen to our mind over heart. The heart they say is a gullible impersonator. It is easily enraptured by temptations. It generally is partial to Easier over Righteous. We have been warned that if we listen to our heart it will definitely lead us to evil, desecration of our soul and eventual downfall. Due to its many vices, heart has been branded as a snake oil salesman over centuries.

Let's look at the counterpart- Mind or the Brain. Mind they say is the steadfast sibling of heart. It is a rational evaluator, blessed with the luxury of wisdom and experience. It is said to always give the correct judgments and aid a human in making informed decisions. The mind will always choose the Righteous, however cumbersome it may be to follow. So our ancestors expounded, that listening to the mind over heart will always benefit us, though it may not be as enjoyable.

I BEG TO DIFFER.

I do not believe that the heart always opens the doorways to doom, while the mind is a precursor for enlightenment. Allow me a minute and I shall prove it. Pardon me for creating an illusion to put forth my point of view.

Let us imagine a scenario. All of us are the "I" in the following demonstration.

I am driving up a mountain terrain, amidst torrential rainfall. The water is pouring over and nature has unleashed its formidable fury. My road, or whatever is left of it, threads around a river which has given over to flood. Now as I behold the scene of destruction, something caches my eye. It was just for a fraction of a second, but I definitely saw a flash of red in midst of the black waters. My eyes began frantically scanning the waters again, for that red apparition. Now I see it clearly. At around two arms length from the very edge of the road, a little child is clinging for dear life to a rock, which is tottering precariously against the force of water. It was her bright red sweater which had caught my attention. It is clear from the rush of the stream that her source of support would not be able to holds it ground for very long and the inevitable is bound to happen. She would be washed off and never found again. Erased completely. The mere thought sends shivers up my spine. Now, I can rescue her. Though it would be a daunting task- the bank is slippery, the water is ice cold and the torrent is extremely powerful. It could mean a risk to my life and none of the two of us might emerge alive.

Now members of the Jury (*Heart and Mind*). You have heard all the vital points of the case. Let us hear your verdict. I would appeal my readers to answer to themselves in an unbiased way. What would be the decisions of their own hearts and minds?

Heart says (*or at least a good heart says*)

Whether the risk be more or less, it is imperative to strive for the rescue of a human life. This victim being a child, the moral responsibility adds up. A human life cannot be just given up without fighting for its survival. There is a risk, but I will not be able to face the shame if the child dies and I remain a mute spectator. I am scared though, I won't lie. It is a dangerous situation, but look at the poor little angel. I cannot bear to let her go without making an effort. I have decided now. I shall go and put all my energies and efforts to save the child.

Mind says (*Practical and calculative*)

Hmm……..I have totally assessed the situation. The chances of the child getting washed away are 100%. If I jump into the situation, her chances of survival may improve by just 5%, but the chances of my mortality will shoot up to 80%. Here I am, safe and my survival is almost guaranteed. It is absurd and foolish to risk my life for the sake of the task, which has minimal chances to success. We may survive by a 5% chance, but that is a possibility, not a probability. Odds suggest that we shall both get perished and it is advisable to not take any action, as the loss of one life is better than two. It is despicable, but the right course of action.

Any rational chain of thoughts will suggest the 2nd option, but what about conscience. We are human beings, not machines. We can calculate like machines, but they cannot be compassionate like us. Our mind is rational but heart is what makes us human. Heart is what protects us from becoming monsters. The human who shall jump into the current to save the child and lose her/his life, would be a million times more of a human than the one, who shall walk away from the scene. The instant we stop being human is the instant we lose all our happiness and peace.

This does not mean that we should blindly follow the heart and ignore our brain. The world rests on equilibrium. The heart is equipped to search for and lead the master towards achieving happiness. We have to have it under a leash, so that it does not go astray. A true balance between the brain and heart makes us human. Think with your brain and feel with your heart. Balance the agents and then decide.

XXI

HAVE FUN WHILE YOU CAN.........

Now I would like to bring up a controversial topic. We have been taught over ages that the path to greatness is tough. We have to suffer to achieve something big.

Fine.

Accepted.

We do need to face hardships, give sacrifices and learn to endure to achieve true success. I am with the teachings until here. Whatever troubles we have to face shall indeed come in our way. We shall have to bear them and choose. Choose to bend or break. The point where I refuse to accept these teachings is this.

Since ages it is being pumped into our brains that to become great we should forgo things which make us happy. In the name of self control and reigning in our senses, it is advocated that we do not indulge in things which give us pleasure. In fact we should make ourselves suffer. We should deny our body the joys of life because they are demeaning and will lead us to evil. Though these so called theories are being ignored more and more now days, still I find an enormous number of people trying to achieve greatness by hurting or denying their bodies and embracing sufferings.

The world as it is bad and life is cruel. Whether you like it or not it shall not leave you without making you suffer. It shall squeeze out all from you in return for anything it bestows on you. Everything does come with a price tag. So when life itself shall offer us the honor to suffer and feel bad why should we for one go around looking for ways to make ourselves suffer? Denying little pleasures in life shall only turn us into a miserable human being, who's misery is infectious and spoils days, weeks or lives of those around. Misery is something akin to passive smoking. It harms the people who surround you more than yourself.

How often have we seen rigid, uptight people who swear by rules and regulations. Neither do they, put a toe out of the line themselves nor permit others to do so. Now if you have also seen such people, think back and tell me. How many of these people could be labeled as happy? They pretend to be happy in their little cocoon of perfection but all that is sham. We are human beings. We are never happy if we are not free enough to let our hair down and forget who we are, once in a while. Life is meant to be enjoyed. Rules are meant to be broken.

I do not say that become a felon or a criminal. But live a little. Spice up your life. Take a day off from work, suddenly, without any reason and spend the day at home. Call up an old childhood friend and surprise them. Do something for your partner or lover you never do and they complain about, but do it unexpectedly, unannounced and sweep them off their feet.

I absolutely do not AGREE that denying ourselves small and simple pleasures or saying no when the heart is screaming out 'Yes', will make us any greater than we already are. In fact it will make us an anti-social pest, whom people avoid inviting to their parties. Deriving joy from every moment possible is not evil. It is divine. The only thing is that joy is ethical, morally correct and does not hurt anyone else. Time for an example-

You are a young single human. You see someone at your workplace for instance (*Colleges are also workplaces; we do work there don't we*). You like that someone. You watch them every day. What to do now? Go and speak to them. Put your best foot forward. What shall be the worst that may happen? She/He may say no. Fine…that's it? She/he won't eat you. Heavens won't fall, sun won't start raining fire and you will not wound up alone in the end. At least you won't have the grudge in your heart which comes moments to years later and says- 'What if I had asked her/him once? Life could have been different.' She/He said 'No'???? Too bad. You might feel a twinge of annoyance, but that's it. You move on.

They say that when we are about to die (*and if it is not sudden*), our mind replays the highlights of our life. We always regret the things we never did rather than the things we did. Even so if the things we did, got us into trouble while those we avoided kept us safe, we still wish we would have done those. Now you are free to explore other pursuits. It is off your mind now. Otherwise it was stuck like a boulder to your feet. You were carrying the burden everywhere. Now you are free. But what if she/he seem to be interested. Your life has taken a swing for the better now. For the moment it is beautiful. And that is all we need. Living in the moment.

Never, ever load up a budding relationship with all the baggage from the future. It will get crushed. Let it live, breathe. Take it as it comes. By living in the moment I definitely do not mean to ignore the future. Do not squeal- "*what about being prepared?*"……. "*what about the story of the squirrel and the winter?*".

Let me explain.

A small digression in respect of FUTURE

Two kinds of people are never successful in the world. Those who never plan for the future and those who plan too much

and too early. A certain bit of vigilance is required. Proper,
measured, adequate vigilance. You do not achieve anything
by reaching before or after time. You have to be spot on. Plan
as much as is practical according to the present scenario.
Do not make castles on clouds. Plan for the winter only
when it is round the corner, not when it is ages away.

Living in the moment is fun, it is easy and it is in no way irresponsible. I cite an example from my childhood.

I had a friend who was an extremely diligent and efficient scholar. Always working hard, being prepared for exams and stuff much in advance. Completing his homework in the recess so that he may have time for something else at home. I believe he never got time for that something else.

Would you compare all the recesses he spent completing his homework and all the recesses I spent painting the town blue. Even for a billion dollars shall I not swap my recesses for his. I am happy and extremely content with the lifetime worth of memories; those recesses have provided me with. I am sure completing your homework would have had its thrill too, but I refuse to believe he would remember them fondly, or even remember them at all.

Once we were at an amusement park, a trip organized by the school. Everyone was ecstatic, enthusiastic and downright riotous. It was a great surprise for me when this friend of mine did actually plan to sign up for the outing. I was starting to feel maybe the guy has more in him than meets the eye. While on the trip, we arrived at a ride which involved a water slide at the end that drenched you completely. My heart literally bounced out with joy at its sight and I was on it before you could say 'On'.

Here my friend showed his true colors again. He never got on the ride. Later when I enquired off him as to the reason for his reluctance, the guy replied that the exams are approaching in one or two fortnights. He does not want to hurt his chances at a top five by getting wet and subsequently falling ill. My God!!!!!!! I could have pulled out my hair in exasperation.

offence to the young hearted elderly gentlemen and ladies, I love their spirit of life). He had lost the jive to live. He merely existed for the sake of giving exams, excelling in studies, getting a big fat degree which would lead to a big fat pay cheque. He would keep telling himself at every point in life, that he just needs to get this small thing done and then there would be time to party. Just one more push and then he shall be free. Sadly that push will never come.

He has lost his childhood and half of his youth in approaching that turn where he can relax, but that turn never comes to those who wait. That turn has to be constructed at every point in life. By the time he reaches the stage where he can convince, even himself that it is time to have fun he shall not remain worth having fun. Not because he shall age or something, but because after leading such a long and drab life he shall develop an aversion to fun and won't be able to tolerate it. He shall become a desiccated, tightly wound up person who would regret and complain about each and everything he did not do- not getting on the ride, not having fun while he could.

No other choice of words is truer than the following "Have fun while you can".

Please, please have fun while you can. Life is short and full of crap. It is up to us to make it beautiful. This is what living in the moment means. It does not mean dereliction towards the future or present duties. It just means that we are able to squeeze out every moment of the last drop of happiness it can offer.

Like someone? Go and talk to them. Appreciate the sweater your colleague is wearing? Compliment her. She will feel happy and so will you. Feeling like you are stuck in a rut? Take a day off for no reason whatsoever and break your bed. Feeling blue? Get out and go to the noisiest disco in town and dance your troubles away. Weather outside is beautiful? Go for a drive. Take the highway, and pull your partner with you (if need be kidnap her/him). More about this on the other side.

XXII

TAKE A DAY OFF

Now some of my friends may react negatively on the advice to take a day off just like that.

It is not shirking work or escapism. If someone does that they are actually helping themselves and the place they work in.

Suppose you are down and in no state to work. But you are a 100% attendance, kind of a person and you detest taking days off.

So you pull your sorry self (*please feel free to substitute "self" by any other word*) to your workplace and start the daily grind. To begin with, your efficiency levels are just 40%. You shall take more than double the time to finish any given task. In addition your diligence levels are at the minimum so you shall complete the task in a half hearted way and the results shall be sub optimal. On top of that you shall be a menace to the people around you. You shall unnecessarily crib, shout, moan, complain and pull faces. If you are in a job that requires public interaction this could be extremely hazardous. You shall miserably drag through the day and keep waiting for it to get over.

While coming back you shall recollect all the sorry incidents of the day further depressing you. The depression may give way to frustration and anger. The anger has the potential of turning into rage when you are driving back through the peak traffic hours. You become an electro magnet for all the despicable and negative vibrations in the environment. Hazard after hazard.

Let me leave the story till here. Now imagine the reflection.

If you had actually taken the day off it would have been, if not enriching at least free from all the negatives you collected. You might have stayed home, got up late from sleep. Getting up late in the morning at least once in a while is also a good but extremely infamous practice. When we exert and exhaust ourselves the body needs rest. If we are not able to provide adequate rest the fatigue is not removed completely. The residual amount of fatigue stays inside the body. Next day when we wake up, will power enables us to jerk off this fatigue and begin the day anew. But however much active we appear, the fatigue stays inside our muscles. The new day brings new waves of exhaustion which adds on, like sand in an hour glass. In the interval between the days of the week, we may not be able to rest for adequate amount of hours needed to re freshen ourselves. The residual amount of fatigue remains and retards the optimal efficiency of our body.

An odd day off from work provides you with the chance to fulfill the quantum of rest needed to remove this residual amount of fatigue. Hence comes waking up late from sleep and its efficacy in improving our efficiency to work. A sudden unplanned, surprise day away from work is like a welcome change. It is like a bolt of lightning but that which does not harm anyone. This is one of those unplanned things which are always welcome.

Do not get me wrong. I am not advocating shirking of work or turning away from responsibility. These casual days off should never be taken when you are aware that some essential work is under way or your absence shall have a negative impact. This day is for self rejuvenation and thus should never be used in a way it hurts someone.

What to do on this surprise holiday?

It would actually stun many people that when they do actually take such a day, after an hour of leisure they are at a loss, as to what to do with it. Workaholism (*there was no such word in the dictionary while this book was being written*) has been deeply ingrained into their habit. They might start getting irritated and instead try to fill up the day with some alternative piece of work. It is absolutely your wish how to spend this day. The objective is not to keep you away from regular work. The only objective is to keep you away from regular life. Change. The spice of life.

If you are not fatigued and feel equal to it you may choose to work more strenuously than a regular day. The only purpose of such a day is to remove you from your constant orbit and make you dance to a different tune. To take you away from the same place and the same faces and the same routine. Everyone needs to do that once in a while. We never understand how much we miss someone or how much we are used to someone, when that someone goes away. At your workplace or school no one is your family or related to you (though not in all cases). But this theory does apply to these places also.

It is not only about anyone missing you or not, it is also about you missing the people or the place. Also human beings have a funny tendency. When they are close to a certain individual or spend a large amount of time with the individual they tend to find too many faults with them. It is basic human nature. Every now and then it is essential to give others the space they need. Why to let them take you for granted. Whatever you do for them is accepted with criticism. Move away for some time and let them fend on their own. They should realize the importance of what you do meekly. When a small cog falls off the whole machinery breaks down. The individual work of that cog is never valued but what is to be realized is that its action is as or more imperative than any others.

So all in all, a day off is a good idea. Day off does not only apply to work or school or such. It also applies to family. There comes a point in every family (*and this point keeps coming back regularly*) when every member of the family is irritated (*or pissed would be more appropriate*) with everyone else.

These are the perils of living together. Human beings as social animals have been designed to stay together but every once in a while they do need their own space. If you try smothering with love at such a time it shall be only more damaging than healing. The best policy is Day off.

Give each other space. If possible take an outstation trip of a day or two and cool your heels. Hang out with your close buddies at such a time and if the other members do the same it shall be extremely helpful. Contemporary company is extremely essential for every human being. We all have family but there are lots of things one cannot share with their mother, father, even wife. We need a buddy of the same age and situation to share our grievances with. Talking heart to heart and uninhibited. Saying things we never said to ourselves. The process acts as a washing machine for the soul and mind. All the negatives are rinsed out and we feel light. We emerge from it content and doubly fond of our loved ones.

I have experienced it first-hand.

There was a friend who was having a certain amount of discord with his wife for some time now. Their frequent quarrels were maligning their relationship. They had issues like every couple but the paradox was that they were deeply in love. My friend was at his wit's end. Fortunately and unknowingly I served as an instrument in helping them re discover their love for each other. I had to make a two day trip to another city for business and he decided to fall in with my plans. Those two days of separation between the couple acted like an aphrodisiac. When the trip began he was insanely happy at having gone far away from his home, the place which was taking away his peace.

After two hours of revelry he started remembering his wife fondly, after six he couldn't stop talking about her, after a day he was professing his love for her and his fortune on having her in his life. I could barely keep him put for another day and when we landed he rushed into her waiting arms. She was even more ecstatic to see him. They separation had healed their hearts. Sub consciously their softwares had been restored. The time of isolation they found provided them an opportunity to re-assess their lives.

We take a lot of things for granted in life and those imperative things start irking us off. That is normal human nature. When they were constantly together they did not get this opportunity for looking into their own selves. A small span of time, a few hours which they spent away from each other did just that. Initially when they just moved away they felt a surge of relief and a guilty pleasure of riddance. They celebrated the fact of having the chance to spend a few moments of calm from the accursed company of each other. Isn't this shameful? Not at all. It is natural. Everyone needs their space. Our lives are not going to provide us this space themselves. We have to understand our own psychologies and plan a get away from time to time, to provide this 'Space' to ourselves and others around us.

A small digression in respect of CHILDHOOD

Do we not remember that there used to be a time
in our childhood, when we sincerely wished for our
parents to go out for some time so that we could enjoy
at home, alone? That never meant we did not love our
parents. We just needed to restore our softwares.

Coming back to the stages during separation. Once the person has experienced that guilty pleasure of riddance they start to feel pangs of loneliness. This is not the loneliness which can be cured by going to a crowded place or even meeting close friends. The cure to this loneliness lies with that One and only special love. That amazing sensation of support and completeness we feel with them. Funny isn't it? We never feel lonely when we are with the person we love, even though we maybe on an island, while away from them we feel lost. The pangs of loneliness are also accompanied with tremendous amount of guilt, guilt at the pleasure we had felt when she/he went away. The guilt at the thoughts of hatred we felt towards them. Again perfectly natural.

Do not feel that you are a horrible person if you have gone through all this. This is all a part of healing. It is a cleansing process. Guilt is good. This guilt and loneliness give way to a surge of extreme love and adoration. Recollection of fond memories. We reminiscence how she/he had done something absolutely unexpected and wonderful for us. That surprise birthday party, that romantic dinner, that midnight walk on the beach, that sitting up by bedside all those nights, when we had been sick.

Never shy away from reminding yourself of these things. These memories are powerful motivators. They turn us into strong human beings. It is very easy to remember horrible things, in fact it is extremely tough to escape from the clutches of bad memories. But bad memories do nothing more than destroy our conscious. They are dangerous for our soul. They attract negative. The surge of love is followed by painful longing. Longing to be with her/him again, with a resolution to never let go. Of course this resolution shall be broken soon, but it is still worth it. This resolution is borne by such strong emotional and amorous feelings that it is almost sacred. That is the most wonderful thing in the world- two people, in love with each other, madly, insanely and infinitely. Once you have felt all this-

Congratulations..........your software is updated. The healing has been done. Re-unite with your loved one, but remember this is not permanent. Please remember that next time, take this self-intervention before things start going out of hand. This is such an easy process and so essential, yet so under practiced. Lots of relationships have been sacrificed but for the need for small measures which could have saved them. It is always easier and favorable to mend. Always a cause for celebration, because once things fall apart, it becomes impossible to join them. A string is beautiful only until there is no knot in it. Knots are fatal for relationships. Mend. Sometimes we need to go far to come closer.

XXIII

WHAT DO I DERIVE, WHEN I DRIVE????

Industrialization, prosperity, wealth, urbanization and affordability. Aren't these awesome words, music to the ears? The country called India is in a transition phase. It is in a trans................or should I rather say it is in a Trance. Whatever they say might be happening to the economy, the exchange rate of currency or the stock market, that whatever has not taken its toll on an average Indian. I see all this hue and cry, only on the sordid projections of the news channels. The mass media has certainly succeeded in reducing a serious job as reporting news, to the travesty of a soap opera.

The Elitist says-

Probably, the well groomed, decked up and suave news hosts are the only ones, who are bothered about the rising prices. I say this because, I do not see anyone out on the street too much perturbed. They may echo these thoughts in discussions, Government bashing and in light tete-a-tetes, but otherwise seem quite smug. Ask anyone and they would curse everything around for the fall in their profits. *"Business is not what it used to be. I used to carry bags of money to the bank, all that is in the past now"*; exhales Mr XYZ while nodding his head in mock despair.

What about that shiny new red car of yours parked outside your swanky 5000 sq ft showroom eh? The average Indian has become a richer man. The new Indian can afford a lifestyle which her/his forefathers only dared to dream of, that too on particular festive occasions. This is a critical paradox of Today's India. It may be tagged as a poor country by the Big Four, but the people residing in it are rich. The lifestyle of an average Indian is far more lavish than that of a hard working average citizen in one of these superpowers. An average Indian today has a lot of things.

First and foremost every city dweller, each and every single person, every nincompoop, every tom, dick and harry, owns a Car in India. My God! It's mayhem. The chaos is unimaginable. A four wheeled vehicle has become a joke. Gone are the days when-

> *You used to feel the lust of conceit and an*
> *overpowering superiority complex and your*
> *neighbors would burn with jealousy*

because you owned a "CAR". Vice versa may have been the scenario easily, so please feel free to imagine yourself in the shoes of the neighbor. Even those days have gone when you could afford the sin of vanity because you owned a Biiiiiig Car. It is not a biiiiiig deal now days. Everyone has it, no one cares and "*So what??????*" is the attitude. Statistics reflect that in the city of Delhi, the number of cars is equal to the number of families living here. Once upon a time, India was sneered upon by the west (*still is*), as being a land of snake charmers, rope tricks and brown people. Lots and lots of brown people, exploding with people, people everywhere. Welcome to the new India. De board your flight, collect your bags and stride into a metropolitan city to discover the true delight.

Enough of Elitism

People plus unimaginable number of cars. Four wheeled monsters everywhere. Cars at the traffic lights, cars racing on the roads, cars snailing through the traffic, cars parked in some of the most whacky places in wackier positions, cars honking blaring and literally screaming, cars weaving in and out, cars being driven in such manners which would shame the machine on its invention. Any peak traffic hour, in such a place, is literally Hell on Earth. I have frequently marveled at the fact that I haven't till date had a heart attack, when I'm stuck in this apocalypse. It seems that every scrounger, loafer and loiterer has got behind the wheel to extended his (*I shall use only 'His' here because this is not a feminine vice*) personality onto his car. Their cars behave like them, bullying and being mean. Every day many battles are fought on the roads. Battles of wits, battles of egos, battles of classes, battles of residential areas, battles of car sizes. Though, no one may admit but the aggression and blood boil at such a situation may be equivalent to that on a real battlefield. People are affected a lot by what goes on the road. Their moods, work efficiencies, demeanor and lots of other things hang on it.

SCENARIO

Someone cut a guy off badly and the poor dear had to screech and swerve away, to avoid a collision. The perpetrator is driving off to the top of the line. The victim would snarl in mad rage and mutely declare the ba****d as his worst enemy and swear vengeance on his blood. People on the road are often described and remembered by the color and model of the car they are driving. Let's say the villain of our story is a- "Black Martini" (*I've never heard of any brand of car called Martini,* *this is entirely fictional, I do not want copyright issues on my back so soon).*

The "Black Martini" would achieve a spot in the blackest part of our protagonist's heart. He won't rest until he zig-zags his vehicle, over speeds and endangers his and others' lives, to get equal to the Black Martini. If successful he would get behind or aside the enemy and honk with such force that would break the horn. It is, as if the power of his hatred is surging into the horn and shooting up its decibel levels. The horn itself should be capable of blasting away the enemy. He would vent out some assorted profanities like-

"How Dare 'He' cut 'Me'? Doesn't he know who I am? I shall burst him into a thousand pieces with his joke of a car. Huh! Look at the loser's taste, he has bought a @@####@ car, piece of sh**."

At such a time, most of the people wish to be immediately blessed with certain select superpowers to quench their thirst for revenge. The super Power to- lift and throw heavy things, to burn objects by merely looking at them, and to blast holes into solid objects, are some which are highly coveted. Alas!!! all these fantasies merely play out in the head. What our victim does is swerves wildly, honk deafeningly and then cutting sharply in front of the 'Black Martini'. Payback. Revenge. Getting even. *"If he cut me, I'll Bl***y cut him."* This is one scenario.

The other is that however much our victim tries; he is not able to reach the perpetrator. Getting stuck behind a dolly car or what nots, he is never able to avenge himself. He is left fuming in emasculated rage, grinding and gnashing his teeth. This is an even more dangerous predicament. Now the rage would be converted to bitter bile, which would be spewed intermittently, throughout the day or maybe two, on everyone in vicinity, scalding and hurting them. Unexplained anti-social behavior and mood swings.

Please tell me- Is all this worth it? Why are we letting our imaginations fly away with us? A car is a car and the road is the road. Come out of this delusion of grandeur. We are not kings, big shots or rulers. The root of all these problems is ego. We spout all the negativity in our blood, on the road, behind a wheel, because that is one place according to us where social graces do not apply. We feel that it is a race track, where everyone is an equal. We would not have to bend backward, or swallow our pride because someone is our boss, our elder or our obligator. Emotions like jealousy, frustration, insecurity, dissatisfaction heat up and amalgamate into RAGE.

That rage is taken out on fellows, who are on the road simultaneously and the irony is, that no one is ready to cool down the tempers. I have never ever seen a single person trying to pacify the tempers in such a situation. Ladies, I am sorry, but I have seen that you are frequently the ones, who add fuel to the fire. Given your grace, delicacy and feminism, this is not something which is expected. Road rage is serious and a good many people have lost their lives, health and sanity to it. Ideally it should claim zero victims. Road is a place where we get our worst impulses. A perfectly sane, pleasant and compassionate person is seen cursing and swearing behind the wheel.

Even he shall get ideas like-
"*I should smash his head*"
"*If I was pardoned one crime, I would burn that so*******ch with his car*"
"*I should start carrying a baseball club in my boot*"

You would be lying if you deny having any such thoughts, at least once in your life.

What to do then. Should we just swallow it all? Next time someone bullies us on the road, should we just look down and take it. How about Anger management..or counting to 10? With all due respect, I believe all this is utter waste. No one ever benefited from these sessions and if you keep tolerating, you are just accumulating all the rage to let it out one day in a single explosion. We all know that when we pretend to forget how angry we are, we just try to conceal a raging fire with a bed-sheet. It will keep on simmering and will eventually burn the cover and fan out, maybe hours later in a much more dangerous form than it was. The only way is, to condition our minds to avert itself from evil. We get angry because we feel that the bad driver should not get away with this kind of behavior. We should teach her/him a lesson. But what we need to understand is this-

- *It is about us and not about anyone else.*
- *Teaching him a lesson won't change him because his state of mind remains same. He shall repeat it. (Pardon my 'He' please).*
- *Our anger will hurt no one else except us. It shall corrode our insides and rot us.*
- *He is not worth the attention we are thinking of giving him. He does not deserve even a curse from us. There are better things to do.*
- *If in the altercation we are ill used in any way (be sure that will happen), it will hurt our sensitivity and our self respect irreparably.*

I am not saying that we should look away or always avoid a confrontation. This is not escapism. But we should- fight where and when it is worth fighting. Throwing a rock in the mire shall soil your clothes. You may argue for 7 days and 7 nights, for what? The perpetrator shall never accept his fault. Neither will you, if you are at fault. It will not yield anything except being an utter waste of time, energy and psyche. Fight where it is worth and noble to fight. Fight against the harassment of a girl in public, fight against the cowardice which is seen every day amongst the bystanders. Raise your voice and fists there.

I fail to understand, where does all the manhood and machismo vanish away in such a situation? We are ready to tear each other's guts out for a small scratch on the car. But, we do not even whimper when a girl in our country, in our city, in a public place, is treated in a way, even wolves would be ashamed to treat their prey. Channel your energies for the better. If you have rage, use it against those who deserve it. Not to satisfy egos and selfish ends. The proper and channelized use of anger makes it worthwhile. A slim historical figure, who lived covered in a shawl and wore glasses had suggested something similar decades ago. Have we forgotten?

XXIV

BRAND GOD:
RELIGION INC. PVT LTD.

*I*s all propaganda about God, just a myth? This place has probably always been here and run itself, the way we know it to run. Maybe it is all self sufficient and supporting? People are born, trees grow, the wind blows, the Sun and the moon alternate and life goes on. No one is actually needed to guide it to run? And all this Hogwash about God being there and prayers being answered was probably a propaganda for a different and the most lucrative kind of business idea. The business of Godmanship. One of the most lucrative ventures that has stayed forever and influenced the tides of the economic world is the Business of God. God has been successfully metamorphosed into a commodity, a profitable Brand. The most bankable and profitable commodity ever plausible. They talk high stuff that no one understands to establish respect and a tinge of fear. And we do everything they say, get carried away, fall prey to superstitions, perform illogical, idiotic rituals and pay for illogical, idiotic rituals to be performed. The business of God is based on Fear.

A small digression in respect of FEAR

Yes fear. Isn't fear the most powerful motivator in the world. Fear is the king of all emotions. Fear gets work done. Fear is the ultimate masquerader because we never admit that we experience fear. It pretends as other emotions- jealousy, anger, insecurity, grief, and even happiness. Fear has been embellished, embossed and glamorized. It has been covered by hundreds of layers to make it unrecognizable. But the truth remains. Fear is the most basic and emotion of mankind ever since it has existed. We do everything because we fear. I do not think that was our Creator's original plan. She/He probably did not intend that our lives be governed by fear.

People are scared and so they will run to God. God is not accessible (or so they are made to believe) so they shall need an intermediary or an interpreter to reach God, to pour out their woes, to pray and beg for mercy, to demand riches and glory. This intermediary than shall be weighed in gold, so as to put forth the message to God and resultantly the coffers of the bosses shall never dry up. It is like bribing the peon to reach the boss. Yes, welcome to the reality. This is a business and a huge one looking at the turnovers and we all are contributing to this ever inflating monster. The psychology of a human is exploited and those undergoing a rough patch of time are the soft targets. Bad times. Bad times force a human TO----------

Change
>   Do the unimaginable
>>   Adjust to the un-adjustable
>>>   Commit to the unthinkable
>>>>   Agree to the most repulsive

Think about and act on something which she/ he would have vowed never to think or act on

Bad time is a ruthless teacher. It teaches us but charges its fee in tears and blood. It is a malicious schemer. It makes a human do, think and say things one had rejected or disposed off as filth when the days were still gold. At such a time the human is most vulnerable. Like the shield has been stripped and the raw red mucosa lies exposed. Extremely sensitive and fragile. This can be only experienced by someone who has had to bear such a phase in life, precisely speaking- everyone. When the times are bad a person IS------------

Nervous
   Scared
      Conscious
         Jumpy
           Fatally low on confidence and self esteem

Every decision he ever took is rebuked by the world, every blunder that she/he committed is amplified and broadcasted, while the several brilliant decisions he had taken are shoved under the carpet. He is whipped from all quarters of this world (*sometimes literally*) and the belief that he is worthless, is first sown into his subconscious and then watered, manured and provided all the requisites to germinate. His reputation is like the ash, hanging precariously at the end of a cigar. At such point of time a Man or woman for that matter is like and as loved as an inflamed blister. She/He is starving for approval, love, respect or even a shred of polite conversation. Now such a poor devil is also a target of numerous advices. Frequently from the so called well wishers.

Measuring the IQ of these well wishers may not warrant the need for a 3 digit number. (*Ok now I am just being mean*) Do this, do that. Go here, go there. And driven by her/his own despair and in a desperate hope for change the person does follow the advice. In 99% of cases it is to consult a Godman- priest, astrologer, numerologist, ascetic, self crowned enlightened, self proclaimed Gods or the more sinister one's who dabble in dark and occult magic. I name all of them together because they are all different specialists of the same discipline.

[*I would like to profusely apologize to those rarest of the rare members of these professions who are actually involved in social service*]

XXV

GOD FOR SALE

The people who are in this business, know the ropes of the trade extremely well. In fact they have an extremely specialized and professional approach to their bait.

Step I

They are silver tongued. A person who has been subjected to the tongue lashing of the entire world is overwhelmed at the fact, that a fellow being is addressing her/him with such a tender choice of words. Already the person has been moved favorably and has decided that the person before her/him is *Godsent*.

Step II

Nothing under this sun (*or any sun for that matter*) is new. Ever heard of the statement- "history repeats itself". True as gospel. So however firmly we may choose to believe that the grief we experience is unique, one of its kind and immeasurably more than what our peers ever had to bear, it is not true. Whatever we have gone through in our tough times has been repeated multiple times in the history. Now these professional Godmen are well versed with the common kinds of "Bad times" in vogue at a particular span of time. The way their victim carries her/himself, dresses up, body language and the kind of lack of confidence she/he exudes aids them in making a very educated guess regarding the nature of one's problem. Remember you are not the first one who has come to seek salvation at his or her door (*I'll just use His now onward for the sake of ease*). He has heard so many people bleat about their sorrows, that he becomes temporarily deaf and is able to deduct the case merely by a study of the facial expressions (*our local Sherlock eh!!!!*).

First a smile and few kind words and then, the dummy God equipped with the knowledge of all the previous cases and experience, tells you what ails you before you utter a shred of your crisis. You are stunned and relief bursts in the pit of your stomach. Your search has ended. You have found the One you were looking for. Yes! Yes! This is the very Angel you had been looking for and he will definitely deliver you from your troubles. You are sold.

Two steps, two carefully calculated steps, admirably executed and the fellow has you eating out of your palm. Now you are blinded. You will not listen to anything lest it is uttered from his lips. Your wishful thinking has given him the coveted spot for God in your subconscious and you will worship him with all the submission that is mandatory.

Step III

Now the Dummy God, who already has achieved a ground will sprout roots which worm their way in to get a firmer adhesion. He will himself create doubts regarding his integrity and quote examples as to how some nefarious monsters take advantage of poor souls like you and milk them off their money in the name of deliverance. How his heart bleeds at such travesties of faith and he himself will advise you to be careful and alert.

This last was his master stroke and though you had already disposed off your doubts during his 1 and 2, by now you are aggressively thinking of arguments in his favor and ready to shoot them to a less of a believer.

Step III over, the actual game gets over in a jiffy

You are unaware of the fact that you are in the net now that has been woven around you very craftily and the beauty is that you will not even struggle to come out of it. The parasite will suck out from you as per your will and then when you are dry, throw you off. The irony is that you will not wish to be thrown off and will experience abandonment. In this game the prey develops an affinity for the predator. The realization sets in very late. This is the trade of feeding on sorrows. Minting money from a person who has seen the murkier part of life.

Extortion is made on pretexts of prayers, solutions, chants, changing alphabets, prescribing gems, or abominable practices of the occult to harm the nemesis. The more sophisticated ones are also the more formidable ones. They do not even pretend that they have any monetary objective. You will never for an instant doubt their intentions. They operate in such a way that you will loosen your purse strings yourself towards their "Cause". They will paint a compassionate picture before your eyes of the lesser fortunate, of the dying masses, the hungry illiterate children, the homeless and how they are striving to eradicate these evils. So emphatic will be the presentation that you will be ashamed to be worried over trifles of your own and volunteer to work for the Greater good. Also it will be understood that charity will wash away your evils and deliver you to peace.

The infuriating truth is that all this is a big hoax. Those poor children, those homeless, those devastated etc. never get a penny of the advantage which you donate for their welfare. They are just used as poster boys and girls to soften the already bleeding hearts and to force them to cough up. And this fortune collected goes into the already overblown paunches of these ruthless Dummies and their financiers. Such parasites are the worst kind of human beings imaginable. Even worse than thieves who may have turned to unscrupulous means to support their lives, but are openly so and do not wear masks of philanthropy. Worse than corrupt businessmen who use plots, schemes and manipulate and bribe people to make profit. Because everyone knows they do all this to make profit. They do not wear a garb of goodwill or social service. They are ruthless and we know it. But these Dummies are like chameleons. They bleed their victim off, of everything and then dispose her/him off like a spent cartridge. All the while talking highly and precipitating the illusion of humility and aura of sacred around them. The sad part is they cannot do anything without us being an active agent, almost an intermediary in their twisted schemes. Will this go on. Can we tolerate such tragedy without turning an eyelash. The answer lies where all answers lay. With us, within us.

XXVI

THE GREAT INDIAN ARRANGED MARRIAGE BAZAAR

ARRANGED MARRIAGE CHRONICLES

I have searched but failed to discover, any other race, population, clan, community, sect, tribe etc. etc. in the whole world which is obsessed with the idea of marriage to such extents, as our Indian Aunty Jis and Uncle Jis. These Aunty Jis and Uncle Jis are not to be blamed alone for this mania though. Girls and boys are equally guilty. Infatuated, obsessed and crazy about the thought of getting married.

The thought is born, I guess even before the insight is developed. The dream of "the quintessential prince charming on a white horse who will sweep me off my feet", or in case of men- "the blue eyed fair maiden" (*fair as in a figure of speech, no color bigotry*) who is waiting for me. You would be lying, if you refuse to have been intoxicated with these ideas ever. Every one, I repeat, each and every one of us, has devoted blissful daydreams to such notions. The craze of weddings is infectious. It is like a contagious virus. People harbor infinite dreams, aspirations, expectations and fantasies about their weddings. The bar is set too high. This would happen, that would happen.

Since childhood, more so in females I guess (*males never achieve that level of maturity*). The idea of their own wedding is sown very early and sprouts much sooner than the girls themselves have grown up. It is reflected in their behavior, psyche and choice of words, even during their childhood. Hints can be elucidated while watching them play with their dolls. The game of bride and groom must be as old as time itself. The most popular game in the cult of little angels everywhere. This is not merely child's play though. It reflects the basic desire and subconscious information regarding marriage. Though we may not be aware about the specifics of the union of two people, when we are kids, we have a fundamental idea. We just know that it is essential. Even before someone educates us, this kind of knowledge is and has always been there. Written perhaps in our Genes. Woven into our sub conscious. Imprinted onto our very soul.

The craze and excitement to have a fairytale wedding is omnipresent. Like the many famous actresses whose famous characters endorse the fact in famous hindi movies over the time. The world goes around marriage in our country. Literally as well as figuratively. As soon as a couple produces an offspring they start preparing for the day of her/his wedding. The preparations are even more obsessive if it's a 'her'. The excitement reaches a crescendo when the said offspring starts nearing the marriageable age.

This age is one that has been stipulated by the Badey-Buzurg (*the wise aged*), the society, the community, the peers, the colleagues, the auntijis and unclejis, probably by the biological clock too as the ideal age to tie the knot. It is also influenced by a series of co-factors eg. Educational status, financial standing, profession etc. etc. No one is bothered very much by, what the principal factor feels. Because she/he is viewed as immature and devoid of the vast experience that the deciders possess. So here comes the ultimate irony.

You do not consider "The" her/him mature enough to decide on the time of marriage but think they are old enough to shoulder the responsibility of your expectations. As far as in worldly matters "The" her/him is a novice, a spring chicken but in this matter very conveniently is old enough. In fact for some, the clock is ticking away and if not betrothed immediately, some cataclysmic horror may befall them. Fretting and worrying over the marriage of an offspring is like second nature to the Parents.

It would be unjust to say that Mothers are more obsessed with the idea, as I have seen fathers equally and compulsively infatuated by it. The age old generation gap raises its ugly head at such times. Whether the kid is getting married in the arranged fashion (*as is the case in majority of the households in this country*) or has selected her/his own mate. The arranged marriage system is a source of wonder and amusement for the western world as it is unlike anything that ever happens there. The concept of parents searching for a suitable partner for their son/ daughter is laughable to them. In some ways we cannot blame them.................for laughing, that is. Appearance wise it does sound ludicrous. Listen to this.

I am my parent's son. They have decided that the time is ripe for my marriage. They have set out to search for a girl for me. Proposals flow in from various similar families. Similar here means of similar religion and caste, similar socio-economic status, similar "Position in the Society", similar "Izzat and Rutba" (*Honor and fame*), similar ways of earning a living, etc. This is another quite famous concept in the Indian Diaspora. To get married or to have kinship or alliance with similar people.

When these similar people come together, the preliminaries are performed. A basic investigative work-up about the girl and her family and vice versa. The birth details are then sought and horoscopes are matched. In the 21st century, where we live in a world which is crafted by such giant leaps of technological advancement, where a broad mindedness and rational thinking are promoted, it is very sad that such superstitions still exist. In fact they are most rampant in the most modern, cosmopolitan, and urban cities of the country and amongst the highly educated, successful, crème de la crème of the society. Not 2% of them will confess but the keystone factor in match making is the matching of horoscopes. Some 10-15 years ago such superstitions had been practically eradicated from at least the urban society of the country. Today, they are back with a bang in a certainly more ominous and morbid form.

THE SCORING SYSTEM

Both the girl's and guy's families have an unwritten scoring system, when they embark upon the journey of match search. After the familial background has been scrutinized and they are satisfied, the judges move on to the principal factors. They look at the prospective bride or groom in the most critical fashion and score them on the basis of- looks, education, personality, charm, behavior, regard to elders, cooking skills (*reserved for females*) etc. Though everything is ransacked the VETO power lies with the horoscope.

*Everything else can be sacrificed for a good star match,
but the star match cannot be sacrificed for anything.*

They shall will their minds to marry off the ward to a much less desirable candidate, with a good score on the horoscope rather than the perfect girl/guy who unfortunately failed the one test she/he had no control over. Ominous but true. This is the mentality of majority of the neo rich Indian families. So once all the Planets and the Gods in the Universe are satisfied, both the parties decide on a meeting.

The rendezvous of the two families, but more importantly that of the Boy and the Girl. They never say man and woman. Probably because the Boy and the Girl earn the prestigious titles of Man and Woman only after the ceremony of matrimony. This meeting is an exceptionally intense and vital affair. The decision that impacts the lives of two human beings and the circle of people associated with these two human beings is made in a matter of few hours, only on the basis of appearances. If there was ever a higher risk quotient.

Merely on the basis of an hour or two of conversation, appearances and presumptions the decisions are taken in ink, over snacks. And they say gambling is illegal. This is one of the weirdest ceremony in the Indian culture, which leaves me perpetually dumbfound. It is maddening to observe that, the people who are so finicky, that they shall research, scrutinize, compare, quote, bargain, visit 20 different places when they decide to buy a small thing, suppose a kitchen duster; are so frivolous when they have to decide about marrying their child off. A round of applause for the Indians and their gallant hearts, which take such life altering decisions, at the snap of fingers. Some gamblers, gamble for millions, Indians gamble on their lives.

XXVII

THE RENDEZVOUS

During the course of the 'meeting', the parents (*both sides*) reveling on their broad mindedness, hint (*smirking at the same time*) to the girl and the guy to take a few moments of privacy. This, so that they can converse and get to know each other................better. "*Get to know each other*" in a span of 5-7 maximum 15 minutes. This is considered to be an extremely gracious and kind step on the part of the parents.

They are so concerned about their children's' opinions that they have bestowed a full 10 min session to them, to talk and get to know each other, that too at some secluded spot. What more could anyone ask for. That is the way of life. You just need 10 minutes to figure out a person, start falling in love with them and start putting them in that reserved spot in your heart. Jokes and sarcasm apart, this actually happens. You need to give a concrete answer after these 10 minutes. The supreme act of benevolence on part of the parents (*in letting you two meet in private*), has to be repaid and dignified by an answer. The answer should be 'yes' in case their peckers are high. You should have done your home work. At the first instance when the proposal had come in, you should have started looking at the photographs and finding out about the person, if possible from neutral reliable sources. You should have (*this is a new one*) searched the person on popular social networking websites.

These websites are the best places to absorb the gist of a person's lifestyle, social circle and habits. The trick to spy on your supposed spouse through the internet, has gained a lot of popularity now days. Prospective brides and grooms, as soon as they get wind of a proposal, literally screech on to their favorite networking site and use the diligent search engines to spy on the other. In a way this is good as you get to see a more casual and realistic image of the person, rather than the made up, adorned, and bejeweled description you get the other way. I really feel for the poor lambs stuck in this situation. The overt display of literally painful enthusiasm on the part of the parents does not let them take a rational decision. Generally they become so overwhelmed, that they just go with the tide. In a way, it is such a blissful atmosphere that it is hard to resist saying "yes".

GIRLS NOT ALLOWED

Ok, the next few lines are for guys only. Is there anything better in the world than taking a girl with you, to make conversation with her, WITH the express permission of her father? Striding shoulder to shoulder with a girl and guiding her to a table for two, with her father not only willing, but beaming with pleasure, at the two of you. Are not these words sugar when they are spoken- "*Son, now I would like you and XYZ (his daughter), to take some time to get to know each other. Please go and sit away from us, we shall send your coffees there only.* :D :P ;) I am pretty sure the girls feel the same.

OK GIRLS, YOU MAY READ NOW

Let us imagine a happy scenario, whence it is a "yes". After the 10 minute tete-a-tete, the waiting families pounce on the couple (*would be couple*) like wolves. The would be's are taken to separate corners, generally by the mother and conversations take place in hushed voices.

"How does she/he seem like?"

"Does she/he talk well?"

"Do you like her/him?"

"Should we take the further steps?"

The "Yes's" from both the sides are met with a literal uproar of emotions, pandemonium, flurry of phone calls and mountains of sweets and gifts being exchanged. These are not the gifts or sweets which change hands later on. All this is arranged for, at the instant, stat. Who says India is a poor country, where naked and hungry people live? The amount of money spent on this mere meeting, is at certain times more than the whole wedding budget in a western country. And this is just the beginning. Any reasonably positioned family in this country hosts a minimum of three functions that lead up to the wedding and at least one after that. Pomp and show, display of wealth and power. The venue, the caterer, the decorations, the organizer, the flowers, the groom's wardrobe, the bride's outfit and jewellery, the guest list..............................these are all considered as status symbols in the Indian horizon. Who came to who's wedding, who's wedding saw the who's whos of the country, how much did he spend per guest? Such notes are compared, to evaluate the wealth quotient of the host. Unofficial report cards are made and discussed by the wedding guests and a comparative analysis takes place with the last attended wedding. People of India take great pride in their Big Fat Weddings. Apart from an occasion for show-off, glitz, glamour, food, best wines and socializing it serves as a tremendous business opportunity.

MARRIAGES ARE GOOD FOR BUSINESS

Weddings are the gold mine for the Indian business community. Everyone from a humble bell hop to a swanky 7 star hotel owner makes a fortune. So many people get employment and multiple trades flourish during the wedding season. If we start making a list it won't be brief- clothes, flowers, food, jewellery, lights, sweets, gifts, wedding band, hotels, farm houses, resorts, photographer, furniture .... Most of these things are purchased by all the guests attending the wedding rather than the principals involved. Now it is starting to dawn on us why weddings in India are such a joyous affair. Other than the obvious glee of the people involved, they offer so much, to so many people directly or indirectly. Directly to the guests who get a chance to let their hair down and experience a welcome change from the daily rut of life. Indirectly to those people who are in some way, big or small involved in the business of marriage and earn their livelihood through it.

XXVIII

THE INDIAN LOVE MARRIAGE

To this day, the Indian love marriage has not earnt, the respect and dignity of an arranged marriage. The topic is still sneered upon and no matter how cosmopolitan we become, the love marriage is still a sort of uncomfortable institution. Notwithstanding love marriages are emerging increasingly in both the urban as well as the rural setup of the country. Yes, this is a myth that it is only an urbane concept. It is as common, in fact sometimes more so in the rural parts except, that these matters do not come to the public notice as rural areas do not enjoy or rather have to bear the constant glare of spotlights like the cities.

The term 'Love Marriage' has actually been coined only for the sake of our and similar countries; because there is no other way to get married in the West. The Indians call it the love marriage when, the child expresses a wish or declares her/his decision to marry someone she/he has chosen. The parents do not have much say in the matter and unless they decide to take it into the rough weather, they usually agree. Even today when the gossips fly at a kitty party, the love marriage of the son or daughter of a friend or an acquaintance is discussed (*usually behind her back*) with many smirks, sneers and savage taunts. It is not such a big deal as it is made out to be. Most of the times, differences occur because of clash of egos, generation gap and a struggle of who dominates whom. I have in fact seen evidence that approval of the prospective partner is generally the least of the problems.

Though the problem seemingly stems from the instant the daughter/son declares the idea of marrying someone of their choice. Sometimes they introduce the parents to the princess or the prince, while at times they just mention regarding someone who was already known to the family as a part of the friend circle. The thing which creates doubt is, the basic human nature. It rebels against a thought that has been planted in its brain, for execution by a younger or relatively inexperienced person, especially own child. Hurts the ego. This is the road block in majority of the love matches. I say majority, not all. Some parents are so warm and understanding, a bit too much for their own good. Even when faced with an unsatisfactory choice they do not dissuade their child. They have an open discussion, try to explain, put forward their views.

SOME SERIOUS STUFF REGARDING PARENTS

We should remember that they have the wealth of experience which helps them judge a person better than us. They see what we over look or are simply unaware about. The views of the parents should never be ignored even though criticized. We may feel rebuked or belittled by their remonstrance, but when the dust settles the universal truth reigns. Parents can never think ill of their children. If you know them to be thoroughly understanding and open minded people and they are raising some doubts on your choice for a life partner pay heed to it. I know how we think. The thoughts which go through our mind are-

"They want up in this power struggle"
"Whatever I suggest they have to decline it"
"They think only they have got the right idea"
"They just like to see me squirm and struggle"
"They never trust me and consider me to be immature"
"They are saying this because they want to rule my life"

Believe me, I have also had these thoughts, but such negative thoughts are extremely vitriolic to the sub conscious. Repeatedly I have nurtured such grudges and repeatedly I have been proven wrong. Call me old fashioned, but one should not even think like this regarding one's parents. We are a part of their flesh and blood. They can never denounce us.

XXIX

I'M IN LOVE AND MY PARENTS DUNNO

*I*ntroducing your lover as a prospective partner to your parents. From the moment a love affair blossoms and the couple start getting serious regarding the future, this one daunting thought gives them sleepless nights in addition to the amorous cause. The anxiety of breaking it to their parents. Actually they can predict their respective parents' decision with considerable accuracy in the bud only. The one's who's parents will or can say No, know it well. But wishful thinking and dreams of youth are powerful motivators. The young Indians are probably the smartest breed that has ever been seen till present.

They are born salesmen (*and women for that matter; no pun intended*). They know how to avoid disagreements and unpleasant situations. They put to use a form of 'Reverse Psychology' to get their work done. Let us understand this with the aid of an example.

REVERSE PSYCHOLOGY APPROACH

A boy introduces a girl to his parent or parents in an exceedingly nonchalant way, without a hint of any monkey business. 90% of the times they end up being favorably impressed by her and are themselves the one who will put the idea of a possible future in his mind. If he himself had proposed the relationship between her and him and then introduced her to his parents, odds would have been in the favor of a 'NO'. Remember the rebellious human brain. But now, he has taken the caution of never leaking out a drop of his emotions.

On the contrary, he introduced an extremely virtuous girl to his parents casually. Those parents who are already sub consciously preparing for his marriage. The fact (*not actually a fact, but they are made to believe such*) that he is not romantically involved with her, gives further fuel to the idea. When they suggest such a proposition to him, instead of the other way round, they also experience the giddy satisfaction of having been in charge. It is their decision after all. Everyone is happy. The sly devil has got what he wanted without any bloodshed. No weapons were drawn, no cross fire occurred, no tear sheds, no emotional upheavals. The smart young generation. Involve everyone in the process which ultimately leads to your goal. That way everyone is a winner. A little tweak here and there and a thorough understanding of the human psychology can prevent many avoidable conflicts. I do not see any moral qualms in using this idea. It is neither foolproof nor fail proof but enjoys a higher success rate than others. The others constitute of, of course the traditional news breakers. Pick the parent who is closer to you.

TRADITIONAL APPROACH

BOYS NOT ALLOWED

By and large, mothers for sons and mothers for daughters also. Traditionally and historically, Fathers may have always doted on their daughters, but this is one sensitive topic, where they are not to be trusted on. By default Fathers have been designed to hate their daughter's spouse, lover or mate. So even if your daddy loves you and treats you like a princess and even though you may be the apple or whatever fruit for that matter of his eye (*pick your favorite- strawberries, plums, orange, mango....................*), do not attempt to make a sudden announcement of your intentions. Never introduce him to a man who may declare that he (*this "he" is your lover*) loves you more than him (*this "him" is your daddy*). Your father will flip out. The more he is obsessed with you, the worse shall be his reaction. You will make them the worst of enemies. Try to do it calmly and gradually. And the best person to do that, is your mother. Tell your mother and she shall break it to him in such a way, that bones are not broken. Mothers are the best routers to share uncomfortable bits of news pieces with fathers. They act as shock absorbers and use time as a tool to ensure no one gets hurt. Occasionally fathers play this role when the issue is something which falls more in the Mothers' purview eg. Studies, attendance, detentions etc. but new relationships are something which should be best left to women.

OK BOYS, YOU MAY READ NOW

So catch hold of your mother in her best mood, during the best time of her day. That is easy to spot and kids generally know it very well. Also, poor mothers are very easy to please and melt away pretty soon. Kids, who are experts in weaseling out agreements for their reasonable and obnoxious demands alike, can do this with absurd ease. A little bit of buttering always helps. The breach of topic should never be sudden. It is in a crescendo form and requires adequate build up. Make a nice premise. Though, she would catch the gist in the first five seconds, still, dignify her with a lengthy prologue before the story. Add details (*Women love details and mothers are after all women*), talk from your heart (*a sure shot winner*) and be compassionate and most importantly honest. Never ever attempt to relate fibs. Be truthful and don't shy away from accepting the insufficiencies in your prospective partner.

f we try to paint an decorated and perfect picture of the person, it would instantly strike as fake. The world and the people who reside in it are never perfect. Your mother has seen enough of life, which has repeatedly brought home this Truth. Elaborating a person's virtues with vices is the best way to sell. That relieves the listener of a nagging doubt. Even gold cannot be moulded into jewellery without adding some impurity. It shall become too brittle in pure form. When you are yourself forthcoming with the limitations, the other person does not try to pry and look for the dark spots themselves. An imperfect picture shall satisfy her (*her being your mother*). Otherwise she shall go out of her way, to interrogate you or her/him to scrape up the skeletons in the cupboard. In fact think of 1 or 2 minor shortcomings to relate with the odes of praise. Whether she is favorably affected or not, she shall think about your happiness first. She shall read it in your eyes, and if she finds that you are really happy she would fight the whole world, even herself to get you what you want.

God Bless Mothers!!!!!!!!!!!!!!!

Some of you though may have an exactly inverse scenario at home. To you these words may be sounding shallow and stupid. That means, you would rather tell it to your father. You have a *"Mary Poppinsesque"* Dad. An Angel. No problem. Just follow these instructions with your dad. He shall break it to your mother.

THE APPROACH OF BREAKING IT TO BOTH MUM AND DAD SIMULTANEOUSLY

This is another way. It has both pros and cons. You decide to declare it to them, when they are together. Equal footing. Neutral terrain. No man's land. They shall appreciate you, considering them as equals. Especially, you shall win brownie points from the parent, you are not as close to as the other. Oh! come on, it does happen. We are not equally close to both of them and in case of more than one kid, even parents are not equally close to both or all the kids. Don't be naïve.

When you break it to them together, your less favorable parent shall be more gracious. She/He will appreciate the honor and may have a sudden flicker of affection toward you. But there is a catch. At the same time, the one who adores you or whom you adore shall feel a little nettled. The partial parent would not be so taken in by the idea of being brought face to face with the truth with their partner. After all She/He has always stood by you, covered you and favored you unblushingly throughout. You have robbed them of an exclusive, prior byte. You told them when everybody was told. That may create a little dent initially. Still you should plough on. This approach is as good as they come.

SCENARIO I

Break it calmly and gradually, again enriching it with details like in any other approach. Once the news has been broken, it is assessment time. Once the dust settles, there shall be a clear cut list of points in your favor and against you. Few positives and negatives have already been discussed. One point, strongly in your favor shall be the element of surprise. Both of them were unaware. They had no inkling of this. Their opinions shall be divided. You did not give them the time to have a personal meeting. You did not give them time to gang up on you. You have divided them to conquer. They shall either be forced to blurt out the first thought that comes to their mind or shall stay quiet. If they choose to speak, the risk lies that they may have contradictory ideas.

That would embarrass them a little and strengthen your case. The way you describe the situation, may affect them depending on a lot of factors and higher chances are they shall disagree with each other. That means at least one shall be in your favor. That is more than half the battle won. You have already broken ground.

SCENARIOS II and III

Another scenario may be they both react in a similar way and team up. This is like the "All or None" phenomenon for you. If they team up in the affirmative, that is they say "yes" and agree for proceeding things, it's party time. An early Christmas (*or late or whatever depending on what time of year you do this*), call for a celebration. This is the dream scenario, and believe it or not it actually happens more than is expected. The reflection of this is horrible.

Both of them, your mum and dad team up and agree on the fact that they want to reject your plea. They think the partner you want, is not suitable and definitely not the partner they want for you. This is the most dreaded scenario and is often the subject of nightmares when one is in love. *They said "No". What shall I do now??????????????????????*

Do I pine and waste away

OR

Let time do the healing?

OR

Find someone else and forget about her/him?

OR

Rebel and take some drastic measures?

Each of the alternatives is progressively alarming. This is a situation; everybody wishes and prays never turns up in the course of their love life. It is essentially damaging and needs some extensive and highly tactical maneuvers to obtain a turn around. The people who still manage to salvage their love boat from these tempestuous waters, without any extensive damage to emotions and without breaking hearts are my Heroes. They achieve nothing short of a miracle. You need a combination of tact, emotion, compassion, sense of timing, a shred of cunning and all your convincing powers to the hilt to achieve something like this.

Most importantly you have to stay calm. You are playing for a team which is already 5 points down. There is only as much you can achieve by temper and aggression. The softer and more feminine emotions have an edge here. Girls are more skilled (*naturally!!!!!*) for such a feat. They have the right amount of inner strength and fiber for the task. You have to remind your parents of all the love and all the faith they have showed in you and how you never let them down. How you have always had a good decisive power and flair to select the right things to the point of being a connoisseur.

Do not make the mistake of praising your partner at this point of time. They are already raw toward her/him. The more you go misty eyed over her/him, the more shall you abrade their dislike, until it burns into absolute hatred. Praise them. Compliment them. Remind them what wonderful parents they have been, such inspirational role models who have motivated you to be such a better human being. They have taught you, without teaching, the distinction between right and wrong and that to doubt your judgment shall be a reflection on their own upbringing.

This process may take days and you shall have to mollify them enough, to reconsider your plea. But remember. If you know honestly that your parents are reasonable human beings and despite that they say no, or fail to see good in your partner, even after all these prostrations of love, open talks and discussions. Just accept that- They are right. I know this would seem ridiculous and very hard to digest, but they can see what you can't. What they see, they can assess with their treasure trove of experience. If even after considering it for days with your best interests at heart, they are unable to agree, that means it is wrong for you.

They can bear seeing you get hurt momentarily, but that way, they are protecting you in the long run. They would prefer to give you a moment's pain like a pin prick, so that you avoid a knife in the side for your whole life. In such cases pay heed to them and back off. It shall never end as badly as, when you rebel against them and go ahead with your original plans. Parents have a special sense, a supernatural intuition when it comes to their children. They are just normal human beings otherwise but have almost seer like powers to see happy and warning signs. Whether we like it or not, we should learn to respect this power. Within its protective aura we are safe and secure, outside it, we are left at the world's mercy. The choice is ours.

SCENARIO IV

The Fourth type of reaction is silence. It is the most frightening form of response. It leaves you squirming in discomfort. More painful than a straight "yes" or "no". The smarter parents resort to silence. They do not express any reaction on the news. They shall keep quiet, nod or just let out a "Hmm.........". This approach leaves everything in their hands. They mutely pull the ball into their court. You are powerless now. You said what you had to and by reserving their judgment, they have bought themselves time to speculate. They shall have a discussion amongst themselves, weigh out all the pros and cons and decide. The heartening sign is that, they have not said No.....................................yet. They shall give a rational and reasonable decision. They have evaded the tempting path of acting on impulse and closing the doors. They have, in fact decided to give the matter some thought and decide for the best. Keep your fingers crossed and your behavior at its best. Do not rake up the matter again and again. It shall only annoy them. They will get back to you when they are ready, and when they eventually do bring it up stay very calm. If it is favorable, well and good, if not, then some hard work will have to be done. We have already talked about it at length. The steps shall have to be repeated. Let's hope everything works out for everyone.

We spoke about a lot of rules and tactics and tricks, but I never mentioned the No. 1 Rule. That is-

"There are no rules"

What may work for you may be moot for me and vice versa. No hard feelings.

XXX

DO YOU HAVE THE SE"X" FACTOR????

𝒮hhhhhhhhhhhhhhhhhhh...................................

Ok, here it is. That topic. The same. You know what I am talking about. It's the thing we never speak about aloud. That thing. Ummmmmmmm......... understood? The Shhhhhh........ topic. Come on.................... The same we have been shying away from for ages. Something, which needs to be spoken and talked about on a regular basis. The veiled seductress- SEX!!!!!!!

Getting goosebumps already? What is there, about the combination of these three seemingly random alphabets, which make your heart skip a beat? What is the big deal about S.......... E............ and X.............. strung together and being spoken out, which turns us crimson? Forget spoken, even the word written somewhere has some effect. Gives us wobbles, makes us queasy. If we are in company and especially elderly company, the word makes us squirm and practically wet our pants. We may shudder involuntarily, if it was brought about when we are sitting, for example with an aunt. The speediest reaction to the utterance of the term on TV is, changing of the channel by practically throttling the remote. Come on............................. It's just Sex after all. Nothing alien or weird. It is practiced throughout the world, throughout the species, throughout the time zones. It is probably the most undeniable truth of our lives, but sadly the most neglected. Everyone is having sex. PERIOD.

It is the basic phenomenon of Life. Any life, any life form. It is the godammn reason we are all here and our off-springs shall be, one day. This very instant, while I am pattering away all this on my computer and you are perusing it, with a slight grin or a frown or a seemingly straight face (*sitting, lying down, leaning or perhaps in any posture or position suitable* :P); millions of couples all over the globe are engaging in the most fundamental physical routine of an organism. Sex is a great thing. It is a boon from God to Man. It is miraculous. It creates life or rather it can be utilized when the need arises to create new life. The best part being, that is not the only application of Sex.

According to me, Sex has far more important ramifications than just bringing in the babies. Sex is the uninhibited, irrepressible expression of love, undying love for your partner. It is the act which strengthens the bond of true love and cements a relationship. It is the phase, when you truly give yourself up to your partner and unite with them to become One. The Holy union.

Ok. I know. I know exactly why, at this very moment, that sneer is playing around your face. You are rebuking me mentally for being such a naïve dumbo. You think that Sex has nothing to do with all the high stuff like- love, commitment, union, one man for one woman. Your train of thoughts is screaming words like- lust, hook ups, one night stands, and the relatively new phenomenon of casual sex and friends with benefits.

Well, sadly you are wrong, if you think so. Reality check. Casual sex and friends with benefits is not a new phenomenon. It has been there, ever since humans have been there and have been capable of having Sex (*thus, forever*). It may have been less known, hidden, or simply ignored but has been around. The present explosion of mass media and the Big bang of the online social network have made a lot more people aware about it, than would have been 2 decades ago. Ask your grandfather when he is in a candid mood and he will spill the beans.

Why is SEX, the Shhh...........................word?

The basic reason as to why sex is a shhhhhhhh......................word, despite being the most practiced routine, is that it generally involves no clothes. Brushing our teeth, is another routine, but no one squeals when it is mentioned, as it merely requires baring of the gums and teeth. Practice wise, on basis of frequency, sex may come a few ranks after brushing teeth, but it is such a hush-hush topic because, it involves getting naked. True isn't it?

No. You may argue that taking a shower requires more nudity than engaging in an intercourse. Still it is easily spoken about. Mothers all around the world presently, must be screaming to their sons or daughters about taking a shower. It is not the nudity, it is the intimacy. Sex was not such a dirty word a couple of thousand years ago. Yes, during the times which are labeled as ancient. Actually the "Ancient Times" were the ones which witnessed a much more liberal society, resulting in a significantly low crime structure. Those were the times when no one shied away from calling a spade a spade. People during those times, were not like- the delusional moron, who shut his doors to an approaching flood and hid beneath the cot instead of fleeing. Awareness and liberation are the steps which reduce rebellion and avarice. Diminution of these vices, reduce such libido driven crimes. Sex once was what it is, just Sex. It did not have to bear all the baggage it carries around now. We have or rather our forefathers have, over the millennia, converted it into a blackguard.

Let's take a journey-

Sex is the primary symbol of love. Though, I understand that true spiritual love and gratification of lust are two separate entities, but sex isn't all about lust. Sex involves union of two bodies. It is not just a moment. It is a journey, involves a path, the twists and turns and the destination.

It always begins with display of chaste love. Gradually, it ascends to various levels. The loss of worldly emotions and troubles. Only the sub conscious reigns during a so called sexual high. The mind is clear, the heart is pure and the soul pursues an untraceable happiness. The worries and negative emotions like fear, anger and stress are washed away. The real world seems unreal. A fusion of the conscious and sub conscious terrain occurs. It is a trance like state. The pleasure is actually not physical, it is mental. Supernatural clarity and awareness. Being unaware while being aware. The world as we know it, fades away and a new world is born. Surprisingly, in such a state, the new world seems far more believable and true to reason, than the one in which we usually exist. All this is infused into a very, very small packet of time, probably a few milli-seconds to the most.

The union of bodies is just metaphorical and accessory. The actual truth of sex lies much deeper. We see it, as joining of two bodies. But our sub conscious becomes aware of the union of souls. The thread which joins a soul to another becomes evident and crystal clear. The thread which ultimately leads to the creator. The vision of God. Coming face to face with the One. Two souls become one in this union. We do not meet the One. We become the One. That is what it is all about. To become one. Lots of linguistic puzzles, describe it in various gymnasts of the various languages. To meet God. To meet the One. To become the One. To be One. I am the One.

How do you become the One? Well for starters, do not the two of you become One? Yes you do. Now read the above passage once again. All the levels of sexual crescendo, do they not remind us of certain state? That is the state of the Yogis, the state of enlightenment. Is not meditation done with the same objective?

To see God
  To be with God
    To forget the grind,
      To become the ONE
        To delve into subconscious
          To rise above logic and reason
            To leave behind worldly troubles
              To come face to face with the divine
              To pursue an untraceable happiness

Are these not the "Steps"?

Well, sex also does the same.

God gave the most powerful tool of prayer and the road which led to Her when She created us. (*Why am I calling God she? The answer is somewhere in this book itself*). She imprinted it in our system and left us to explore it and to figure it out. It is not at all a dirty thing. It is beautiful, spiritual and miraculous. It is us, humans who have made it dirty by our deeds, perversions and using it as a tool for gratification of lust rather than satiation of the subconscious.

BACK TO SEX

Regarding Sex, we have gone horribly wrong. It was a practice which could have enabled us to get nearer to our creator and find answers to the interminable questions of our soul. Instead, we have turned it into a dirty, vulgar or obscene and derogatory term.

Sounds foolish, doesn't it? I know, lots of jokes are buzzing around your head right now. I know this because they are buzzing around my head too. :D ☺

CENSORED STUFF

Let's get these out of the way before we continue with the life science. So basically this theory suggests that- We should have more and more sex to be a better human being. Sex makes us powerful and helps us "delve into the subcon...... something" and we get enlightened. Sex gets us closer to God

I need to have sex to see God.

When I am having sex my soul sticks to my partner's. Hey sweetheart! I am missing a little of my soul, about quarter pound. Would you check your soul. Maybe mine got stuck to yours the last time.

Instead of going to the church or temple, I should rock mine and her/his world in the crib. That seems more effective. I am not engaging in anything dirty. I am just trying to elevate my soul, get closer to God, become enlightened, become One. The fun part is just accessory.

I guess that much juvenile banter should be enough. Now I shall explain why Sex is divine?

Before you start jumping at my throat because I called SEX the most powerful form of prayer and a gateway to God, research for yourself. Sex was used as a meditative technique.

Sex has held a very important place in most of the ancient religions or sects in the world. The Egyptians, pagans, hindus. Sex was never a frowned upon term once. The union of a male to a female body was considered sacred and miraculous. Ancient Egyptian priests used to engage in sexual contact with the high priestess as a gateway to God, to achieve atonement of the soul. The female is known to be "A sacred element". She descends directly from God.

Union with the element of God is the pathway to God. This statement holds water doesn't it? The soul search in the moment of supreme lucidity. The moment, when we achieve the highest level of the staircase "The Orgasm". It does take us in a different world altogether, whence it becomes difficult to say with surety which world is real and which illusion. The Holy union, the purpose of marriage, the sacred act which brings life on Earth, which introduces God's life force on to the planet. How can it be dirty? Even if we do not agree with this theory, we can at least agree on one subject.

I, refuse to believe, that the phenomenon which brought me and the people I love the most into the world, is a dirty or obscene process. We are all here because some time some people had Sex. If it was dirty, we are dirty as well and so is our existence. Calling life force dirty is an insult to our whole existence. Come out of the stereotypes. Acceptance is the first step to evolution. Opening our eyes and broadening our minds shall help curtailing the negatives around the subject. It shall help a whole generation develop a broad minded approach, the only way to control atrocities, like those which are being committed now.

LET'S WRAP IT UP WITH A MESSAGE

I know and I am aware that everything is not rosy on this sweet earth of ours. Not everyone is the committed for life. "Faithful" is a rare breed. I am not saying that sex is exclusively for creating bonds with your true soulmate. It can be used as a tool for anything from a spiritual union to break-time entertainment. That does not mean that Sex is a dirty, vulgar physical act which leads people to downfall and away from the path of the righteous. We have been made capable of engaging in sexual contact and we have been given the free will. We can make it what we want it to become. Sex in itself is not good or bad. It becomes so on the type of its use. If today, Sex is a shameful word, the reason is because we have put it to shameful uses.

We can involve ourselves in satiation of the libido, engaging in recreational sex, using it as a narcotic or much morbid, using it to achieve goals in the realms of our career. That makes it a dirty word, a taboo. Something to be looked upon with disgust and attaching shame to its utterance perpetually. The follies of man has maligned the name of Sex. It is not Sex which has led us to downfall; in fact it is the other way round. We have used sex more often for less than graceful measures than the optimum. Resultantly it has become a filthy term now. It is not talked about. Parents shy away from having an open discussion regarding the Biology and physics involved (*also chemistry, no pun intended* ;)), with their wards and rely on questionable sources to feed them with the correct information. These questionable sources are- schoolmates, television, X-rated movies, moronic articles in red books and magazines by nefarious quacks possessing questionable qualifications. Now think, what kind of inaccurate and distorted version of the actual information would be absorbed by a young mind. Are you happy with your ward growing up, on the drug-store psychology version of sex?

Human nature is a bizarre puzzle. It has the habit to rebel. It seeks the thing most dearly, which is hidden, kept in covers or forbidden to be spoken about. If you want a child to seek something with utmost dedication and passion, tell her/him to never ever ask about or try to find about that certain something. Same applies to Sex. Not speaking about it, banning the topic or even punishing a young mind for expressing a natural curiosity on the subject, does more damage than any caning would do. You are yourself pushing the child to rebel. You are ensuring that she/he will follow the subject with rock like determination, but never again utter a word about it to you. You have lost the confidence, she/he had in you. Thirdly she/he shall get a garbled version of the events from an uninformed or malicious or a probably dangerous source. God forbid, if something wrong occurs, the child shall never come to you. This will only worsen your odds.

It is much better, safer and advisable that a ward gets the correct and healthy version of things from a parent or guardian, in an open and light atmosphere. Encourage her/him to ask questions. Be carefully accurate about everything and never accentuate stereotypes and myths. Schools now days are taking up the matter seriously and claim to have specially qualified counselors to deal with their pupils' queries on the subject. These moves are admirable, but it is still preferable, that this duty be performed by parents.

A Taboo, deceases when we start talking about it. It stops being a taboo anymore. When we speak about it, it becomes conversational and ordinary. It loses its dark, grey quality and becomes acceptable or relatively acceptable. The hundreds of years of prudish behavior being passed on as legacies, has made us literally lock jawed about the subject. Coming out shall be a little difficult. Thanks to the extremely cosmopolitan atmosphere around now days, this will not be such an arduous fight it might have been a decade and half ago. Children are already quite educated. They may not know about the graphic details (*many know those too* :P) but they at least, they have a very well informed gist and educated guess about what goes around. It won't be very difficult to get through to them. Reminds me of the joke, where a mother sits down her sixteen year old daughter to talk about sex. The cheeky, tongue in cheek, daughter is quick to rejoin with a- "*Sure mom, what do you wanna know?* :D" Jokes apart, with the rate of sexual crimes and assault going on, it is better you don't avoid having a tete-a tete with your young ones, asap.

The age of maturity has fallen considerably. You shall have to catch them young. What was known to a 15 year old around 10 years back is now the awareness quotient of a 10 year old. The TV and the Internet take over them, much before any other influence does. The power of these mass media giants is phenomenal, almost soporific. They are the new Gods. The platform is so alluring, glamorous and so rich in sounds color and content, that it is like an explosion of stimulants for all senses. You shouldn't feel bad on losing out to it. You can't win, when opposed to such a formidable foe. Cutting the digression short, the only need would be, to fine tune the Sexual awareness of the teens or tweens. Just dot the "*I's*" and cross the "*T's*". They already know, but not correctly, completely or sufficiently. Education coming from the most reliable source like a parent, shall only make them further secure and reinforce a bond of trust, which is the most lacking in today's world.

XXXI

HAVE WE ALWAYS BEEN SEXISTS????

Why is the human race, always referred to as "MAN" in history and future? Ahaa!!!!!!!! This passage may be something of a treat to the palate of my feminist friends. The ignoble question. Why? Oh why is the human race, the Homo sapiens referred to as "MAN", when they are spoken about or referred to in History, science, archeology, study of civilizations, anthropology etc? How often have we come across statements like: "Man is a primate who............." or "Man always had the dream to................" or "Man developed and metamorphosed into..................".

No one ever found it weird? Doesn't it strike a kind of an odd note? Why Man, why not Woman? How would these above quoted statements sound if the reflection had been adopted?

"Woman is a primate who........"
    "Woman always had the dream to........"
        "Woman developed and metamorphosed into......."

No offence, but these statements sound ludicrous. I can't stop giggling, even writing these. They are funny, period. I apologies for being such a blunt axe, but I merely state the truth. Actually these statements are perfectly plausible and logical, because Females are equal, in fact somewhat the better part of the Human Race. They complete Men. Notwithstanding, using the word Woman instead of Man isn't such a good idea in this context. These statements have lost meaning and substance. This is not a dais for feminist crusades.

Jokes apart, this has caused a percolation of a rather disconcerting and uncomfortable stream of thoughts in my mind and I am sure in yours as well. Have we human beings been Misogynists, over the ages? Have we subconsciously, consciously or aggressively strived and succeeded to some level, in crushing the importance, essence and respect of the Female? Have we been like this ever since we have been? The global media blares about the degradation of values and morals, associated with rise in crime against women. Women have lost the respect and adulation they deserve. The modern man has (*again Man!!!!!*) become less sensitive to his delicate counterpart, the fairer sex, the better half. The fall of feminine from a pedestal of respect, is the hallmark of breakdown of the culture. This statement is seeded in the echoes of the Ancient Wisdom as well. The ancient and timeless texts say-

"The place where women are not respected is akin to hell on Earth and sits on the precipice of destruction."

The home, where the female is not given respect forever wallows in the clutches of grief and discontent. This is not a joke. These are in fact scientifically proven facts.

They say, that the modern male has become not disrespectful but downright insensate toward the female. Is it actually true? Is this a new phenomenon, as it is painted? Has this arrogance sprouted in the contemporary male, suddenly? Is it not just a manifestation of a seed that had been in dormant and germination phases, alternating for millions of years? There is nothing new under the Sun. There are just cycles. Everything imaginable or unimaginable has been committed, is being committed or shall be committed in the future. This disgraceful behavior of Man towards Woman is nothing new. It was known even when the times were unknown. Man has always been very diligent. At the start of the civilization itself (*whenever that may have been*) the male understood a fact. Though, he may be physically stronger compared to the female (*most of the times*) he is weak, extremely weak and hapless in every other aspect. The female is an embodiment of tremendous, unlimited cosmic, spiritual and emotional energy. She is extremely powerful. Her body is merely a fragile casing holding a fiery soul, something like encasing the Sun in a giant cardboard box. This inestimable power is not always a boon. It is extremely difficult to bear it. The man can never imagine possessing such infinite power. Even if that power is bestowed, the male is not equipped to tolerate and handle it. In fact it shall scald him.

When, it dawned on the male that his energy was no match to the powerhouse of inferno contained within the other sex, he decided to assert his superiority by the only tool he possessed: Physical power. Strength of the body was used to quieten the sensitive voice of the feminine. An extremely dangerous maneuver, which shall backfire in the end but all the same, effective for the time being. Man became the ruler, the God, the king, the master and received the upper hand in the power game and the woman was reduced to the secondary.

Uncomfortable???????? Don't worry. It is not as bad as it sounds and this is certainly not the reason that Humans are referred to as Man. The balance of nature shall be reestablished eventually and the scales shall tip in a more appropriate position. As is true- these are just phases which come and go. Nothing is permanent.

Coming back to our original question. Why is the mortal referred to as Man? It is not because of the supposed malicious designs of the male race and certainly not because of the docility of females. The answer is in fact extremely simple. Humans are referred to as Man, because Man stands for mortal. Everything opposite to God, Divine and Immortal. Humans are referred to as Man so as to segregate them from God. Man and God. The difference between Human and Divine. Do you see it yet? Yes. Male is Human, Female is divine.

We cannot say Woman because she is not a mere mortal like Male. The term is not a sexist rebuke; in fact it celebrates the divinity of woman. The sacredness. The acts and follies of a Human are always referred to, as been done by Man. Man gets the credit and also suffers the brickbats. It is not said "Woman", or "Man and Woman" so as to emphasize the limitations of a mortal, the short comings of being human and the helplessness in the face of divine intervention. As the female is divine, she cannot be referred to, in this context. She cannot be downgraded to such a level. Though the feminine partakes the destiny with the masculine and lives throughout the history she is unaffected, not besmirched and not actually involved in the process. Why? Because like it or not, Female is Divine. She is a God element. This is why I believe thus.

Why is the Feminine sacred, divine or God element? This assertion does not go down really well at any level. Understandably, the Male Diaspora shall never be found to concur with this singularly controversial remark. But we shall be surprised to discover, that even a major chunk of the females shall find it logically or ethically difficult to agree with. The human being has been known to commit some of the most monstrous and shameful deeds in his day. It is not the Male alone, who has executed such horrors (*though has been a statistically higher contributor*). Females have been equally and at certain events, more involved in perpetuating such atrocities. Crimes which would shame a hardened criminal. Over the years, in the history and texts, there have been numerous citations of evil women and their morbid achievements.

So, how can we believe that the fairer sex is of divine descent, when some of its activities are not even worth being addressed to as human?

The answer raises a kind of moot point. Being a divine birth, or of divine descent does not guarantee a saint's life. A philanthropist's son (*or daughter for that matter*) may turn out to be a penny pinching, blood sucking miser. A kind hearted noble king, may father a spiteful and demonic heir. Saying that a female cannot commit sin as she is divine, is as wrong as stating that male can never commit a good deed because he is human. Neither is true. God resides in everyone and we all carry the divine element or particle. The mere fact being elaborated here is, that the male was made by God and infused with the divine energy, while the female directly descended from God. The reason behind this is astonishingly transparent. We can see it in our everyday lives.

The reason Female is divine is, her power to give birth. The honour to be a Mother. The miracle of creation. These are all prerogatives of a woman. New life can only sprout out from a female body. Only the female possesses a womb, which creates this miracle. God is "God", because of the power to create life and to give birth. That is what makes God divine. So, it can be safely said, that the Gender which demonstrates this power on earth is divine as well. The infusion of life force with flesh is a complex series of reactions, which require a conducive environment provided by the female shell. This power or ability of the female is a mere replication of the power of the Creator.

XXXII

IS GOD A WOMAN????

All said and done, does this not bring us to an extremely potent question? If female is divine, because she can create life and so can God, does that not point to the obvious? Are you not following the same train of thoughts I am following? Does this not mean that God is a She?

She??????????? The Creator a She??????????? Yes very much. I am not saying this in an attempt to win over the fairer sex so as to push the sales of this intended book (*though I may have had a teeny weeny jolt when I wrote this because it may actually help*).

Welcome to one of the most ancient enigmas of the universe. We often wonder about, how God created the human being? Well, God left the answers all over the world. We can see everyday how God created humans. It is the same way humans create humans. God created an extension of Her own and bestowed her with the power to create human life. I strongly believe that God created or gave birth to life on earth and then got involved in the process Herself, by creating two different sexes. The fairer sex was given a certain amount of her power. After the female was created, God created the Man, so as to provide an equilibrium. Though both woman and man are small packets which contain the God particle, the female is divine, while male is not. Man's participation is mandatory for the creation of new life. Without a male the female cannot give birth to an offspring. He contributes, but still the process is only possible inside a womb which he lacks.

The miniature reverberations of what might have happened when life was created are seen throughout the world. Women, giving birth to children everyday. Life being created. What does this mean? This is again an indication. Do I mean God is a feminine entity, or more bluntly God is a Woman? Yes. I strongly believe so. God must be a feminine because the power to give birth to a new life is feminine.

Though we may not know or may not be sure, but we can definitely feel at an elemental level, that the world as we know it, is divided into two basic groups. I say groups for the want of a better word. You may camouflage it as divisions, classes, orders, even adversaries ;-) Whichever suits your palate. Regardless of the thought process we may follow- religious, spiritual, atheist, skeptic or any other, we can all safely agree, that the world is divided into two groups. Our instinct tells us, or probably the lost innate knowledge hints to that. (*We have already had a few words about this Lost Knowledge in "The Nagging Questions"*). Whatever may be the reason for this inclination, we do agree that the world is divided between Women and Men. The female and male. The beautiful and the ugly. (*more brownie points from the ladies ;-)*).

Success is what defines a Man

I say ugly for males not out of contempt or malice. Since the beginning beauty has been a female trait and quality. Men are not beautiful and we don't want to be labeled as beautiful. Since times unknown Men have been known for their grit, work, bravery, intelligence and talents. We never come across the reference of a male historical figure, who was known far and wide for His good looks. The only thing that defines a Man is 'Success'. Even to this day, mother's anxiously searching for grooms for their daughters (In our Indian Diaspora, where arranged marriages rule the roost), do not fret for a good looking boy. This quality is sacrificial for greater goods. Greater goods being- money, success and education.

Now, creating new life has always been a feminine thing. Creation, giving birth, producing a progeny. Only a woman can do that. I'm not saying she can do this alone, but she is the one who can undergo the metamorphosis. We don't have any machine or apparatus which can create life. However many scientific explanations may be there, which profess regarding of inter-conversions of various forms of energies, I still do not understand the concept of life. How come a being is born, with a complete knowledge of how to grow, develop and thrive encoded in tiny ciphers in its own body. Once it is born, it starts moving, breathing and making noises. How come it absorbs the knowledge from the world and develops grows, prospects goals, achieves, fails and then ceases to exist. I am sorry, but the laws of science do not explain all this.

Do we not see the urge to discover a source of energy inside everyone, in fact every element. The World itself, which is uniform in code but disseminated. We can use the laws and rules of various branches of science to make machineries that move, process and build. We have been able to give them a brain of their own as well a.k.a. "Artificial Intelligence". Despite all this extensive knowledge and technology, have we been able to create new life? The element of life, the power to feel and the human heart are probably those mysteries which may never be solved. The divinity of life is reflected in our ability to love and feel. That makes us all sacred.

God has blessed us with the power of miracle. That is the definition of divine. This is proof, that we our divine. God is not to be searched outside in places, stones, churches, temples or mosques. The element lives inside us. We need to search inside. Develop an insight. We have learned enough. Now we need to unlearn. Wipe off the slate. Clear the chalkboard. Drop all the baggage. Go back to the pure state and be ready to accept with humility and calm. Be a child, a pupil and surrender to the master. The master being our subconscious. If we believe this, than the easiest way to reach out to God is to respect and revere Her imprint on Earth. Respect and love women. Bow to the divine. Get closer to God. Be the One.

XXXIII

BIG BOYS DON'T CRY

Crying. Though a simple human expression, crying is a very infamous emotional depiction. Lot of stigma attached with it. People shy away from crying. Human beings have been designed to cry. It is perfectly natural. It as an output, for all the negative emotional sewage. Grief, anger, frustration, depression; these are some of the toxic agents which are produced or infused into our system, when we move around in the world. The habitat in our body and mind is not endemic, but is an ideal habitat for these toxins.

We, humans are more comfortable expressing our positive emotions rather than negative. We do not let them out and thus they stay inside. There is a need to let go these noxious toxins, otherwise they start corroding the sub conscious. The question that arises is how to let them out? Should we speak to someone or share it? That is a good idea, but you shall seldom find a patient and compassionate listener. In today's world everyone is themselves struggling with their own troubles. It becomes a little difficult to overcome those and offer a shoulder to someone else. Here comes crying. Now don't laugh you. It does not mean that we should turn on the sprinklers, the moment things are not going our way.

The first and foremost rule for crying is-

"As far as possible, it should never be done in front of anyone"

The world is harsh and cruel. It does not feel sympathetic or warm toward a person who has broken down, though it may pretend so. The tendency of an average human being is, to tread on someone who has fallen down. When you cry in front of someone, you lose respect, you expose your vulnerable side and you invite them to kick you. Do not for a moment imagine that crying before someone shall earn you any brownie points. It shall only take the situation from bad to worse. No one likes a squealer. They shall come to believe that you are weak and thus it would not be a bad idea to crush you some day. Now, these insinuations sound extremely harsh, but that is the tendency of the people around you. The exceptions are mother, father and only one more person who is dearest to the heart. So, never cry in front of a 4th person.

This is one of the reasons, crying is such an embarrassing affair. Kids (*especially boys*), are laughed at, at school if they burst into tears. Though it is widely believed, there is nothing feminine about crying. It appears that women cry more, because they do it more in the eye of the public. Everyone cries or at least feels to be on the verge of crying. The only difference is, due to the social graces men have to keep it under wraps, which is a great idea.

So, if we are feeling bad and we are alone and we cry, will we feel better? Wish it was that simple.

Crying flushes out our systems. It is like a burst of negativity from our soul and leaves us with a feeling of calm and peace. It has nothing to do with tears, they are just accessories. Often, people (*especially men*) state (*or rather boast*), that they can't cry. Even if they wish with all their heart, they won't be able to shed tears. They are right here. Absence of tears does not mean that these people are braver than others, or have a higher threshold for pain. It is just a way of life. Some people start leaking at every instance, while others never shed a tear. Not shedding tears does not mean, not crying. You may not be able to shed tears, but you can cry very well.

Tears and crying are two things, closely related, but still different from each other. Tears always do not mean one is crying and vice versa. Crying is an internal process without a mandatory external display. When a human reaches the threshold of tolerance against any ill, her/his courage gives way. Generally, we are brave enough (*all in different measures*) to tolerate the negativities we experience in everyday life. But, when our limit is reached, our courage collapses and we feel an overpowering weakness. Everything seems against us and there seems no way out. Our confidence drops to zero and the situation seems hopeless.

This is the first stage of crying.

After this comes the stage of reaction. When humans are driven to such a point of desperation, they react to it in two ways- they explode or implode.

Implosion is when you try to swallow all the pain and suffering and wreck your insides. Implosion is the most dangerous reaction to this situation and sadly this is what we do regularly. Due to the pressures, rules and graces of the society we do not express ourselves outside and prefer to take it all in. Then, we falsely convince ourselves that the evil has passed and we have won over it. This is not true. Our sub conscious has not been designed to give habitat to negative energies. Unless we express them out, they shall never go and keep on piling and accumulating. Keeping the pain inside does not ease it, we just forget about it for the time being. It keeps on heating at the base like lava and one day when we lose our balance, it erupts in the form of a volcano, scalding ourselves and everyone around. Implosion is not a desirable maneuver.

The other kind of reaction that we can show is Explosion. It does not mean shouting, ranting or bursting out of our system. Explosion means, to find an outlet for all the pain and misery and letting it go. If a person has really been driven to the wall, she/he will burst into tears. Tears are a very effective way of letting out the pain. We are free of any thought or emotion at that time. The mind gets a chance to whirl in the lucidity and all the toxic matter is washed out of the soul. You would be lying if you say that you haven't felt great after a session of passionate sobbing. It makes you feel light and takes all the misery away. This is the best approach to relieve oneself. After all, tears are nothing but excreta and if you do not let them out regularly, they shall pollute your system. For those who say they are unable to cry, I repeat again. Absence of tears does not mean you are not crying. If you have been driven to such a state and brooded over it, you have cried. Even if you do not shed tears, remember to let it out by some physical expression. Otherwise, you shall start imploding and destroy your psyche. As far as grief is concerned, explosion is good.

If you feel that you are the happiest you can be and can still talk about it; that means you can be still happier. When you experience the epitome of any emotion, it takes away your power of speech. If you have the capacity to feel more, you can still describe how you are feeling. The happiest man on earth will not be able to tell you how happy he is. Same for grief.

XXXIV

ROLL SOUND, CAMERA……….
ACTION!!!!

Sometimes I really thank the Almighty profusely and feel so much obliged, that She made something called the Movies. Rather, She created humans, humans who thought of displaying moving images of men and women on a big white sheet of canvas for their counterparts, to sit and look at them. What a stupendous idea it must have been? I bow to that sublime genius, who actually thought of such a path breaking and revolutionary concept. Pure brilliance. Though, to be fair, the idea had been around for ages and the advent of advanced technologies merely caused the existing to be metamorphosed and wrapped into a glitzy and glamorous package. What would we do without movies, films, cinema, and pictures? We love movies and I can especially announce this proudly.

We Indians have a deep set weakness for movies. Movies are our lives. We live through them, with them. They make us laugh, cry, fantasize and even fall in love. What can I say, but it is the adverse effect of watching these alluring presentations and that too with such great concentration, which becomes akin to mania. I used to think that I was one of the few who were mad about movies, but you can find bigger and even more psychotic movie buffs in every street of India. Movies have become a lifestyle with us. People take great pride in this institution of our country. We have been for ages, colorful and creative people. Indians have always had a weakness for song, dance, drama and have been entertainers for centuries. We are such overtly dramatic that a little bit of this bad habit seeps into our day to day life as well. If we look back at history, even the Indian monarchs used to entertain themselves by requesting routines of song, dance and theatre from the most popular names of their times. That habit has not changed.

Now, in the times of democracy, when the era of kingdoms has gone, every man is a small king in his own way with a small kingdom at his beck and call. The modes of entertainment have become accessible to everyone. What is better than spending 2-3 hours in a cozy darkened movie theatre, with our favorite screen idols cavorting and prancing around to make us happy? We just do not watch movies and be done with it. We breathe them in and out and they work as a powerful narcotic to our systems. After watching a particularly impressive movie, one remains in that mode for some time, ranging from a few hours to a few days. For example- after an action movie you get a fake feeling of macho, can't stop grinning after a comedy, keep floating in the air (*especially if you are having a love affair*) after a romantic one. Our screen actors are our Gods. Laughable for some, but this is literally true in some parts of the country. In these parts, screen actors are actually worshipped in temples, built for them. Absurd????? Not at all. It is human nature to celebrate the heroes and put them on a larger than life pedestal. It used to happen thousands of years ago in Greece and Rome. All the Gods were actually athletes and Olympians who were celebrated and worshipped as Gods and their idols were erected. If that happens in the present day India for cinema personalities, it is not to be rebuked.

What is the psyche behind the popularity of a movie star? Why do we love them so much, that we start adoring them more than our family and get into arguments and confrontations to defend their honor? Is it the enigma, the mystery or the lifestyle? It must be a cocktail of many factors. They get to lead the life, which every human yearns at a cellular level. They reflect the perfect human being, the perfect way to happiness. Their success, even if short lived, is phenomenal and awe inspiring. Most of the times, it is overnight. A nobody turns into a heartthrob, within a few hours of her/his life. This is the stuff dreams are made of. Every one of us, and more so the ambitious ones, crave for success. Unfortunately it is elusive and pre destined. But, when we see a person achieve that and that too in a grand way, despite our jealousy we cannot help rejoicing. Like the two sides of a coin, the human being constantly struggles with two types of emotions. The dark part would induce jealousy and wish for the downfall of the other, but the good part enjoys it. The result depends on which part wins over.

So, a cinema heartthrob has everything going her/his way. Fans, money, adulation, fame, awards, recognition… …………………..………everything comes in a burst and frequently goes away like that. The beauty of the phenomenon is, that the star trades her/his life away for all these fireworks. Human being is such a rascal, who is never satisfied. When I was a nobody, I craved for fame. Now, when I am a celebrity, I crave for the freedom to walk on the road without getting mobbed. The illusion gets broken. The grass may be greener on the other side of the hedge, but it is realized only when we get to the other side.

Still, the magic of cinema is something which is the powerful, intoxicating and slightly maddening. It has taken the sanity of quite a lot of people. We watch movies for various reasons. The basic ones are, to have a good time, to forget ourselves for few moments, to immerse in the virtual and to come face to face with illusions. It would not be wrong to say that the allure of cinema makes the line between truth and fiction very blurry. The magnitude and the scale at which stories are narrated, provides a true joy to our senses. The costumes, the sets, the locales, the music...............................awesome.

Man is stuck in his daily grind and is fed up of it. He needs a moment and a medium to exhale. What can be a more economical, justifiable and morally correct medium than cinema? Movies take us to a wonder world, or as my friend says- *"They take us to the La-La land"*. Beautiful and serene. A land where everything works out and all are happy. They enrich the taste buds of our senses (*all senses except taste; what an oxymoron statement*). We love the characters, the heroes, our heroines and most of all songs. Music is the skeleton of the Indian Cinema and its biggest bequest is, its songs. I do not think, that there is any situation or instance possible in a man's life, on which a song has not been written in one of the Indian movies. Sometime, I am left gaping at the impunity of my brain, when I am stuck in a particular situation and a song from a movie starts playing in my mind. This song cruelly mocks and jibes at the situation I am stuck in. It was a slight shock for me to realize that many of the people, who throng the movie theatres, do it for the sake of watching and listening to their favorite songs on the big screen and bigger speakers. These songs once comprised of running around the trees, but now they say that is not the case. Believe me, it is still running around the trees. And even if it is, what is wrong with that? It is quite a funny way of expressing one's love.

A big chunk of (*or should I say 100% of*) the female population watches movies to scrutinize the dresses and costumes worn by the various actresses and actors. Actresses, so that they can emulate and adopt their styles. And actors, so that they can make their partners emulate and adopt their styles. Movies are always the ideal stage for showcase of the latest trends and fashion in vogue. Whatever is displayed is already a hot property, and if not becomes a hot property soon as it is displayed. To depict the power of this medium in a humorous way, once a celebrated actor put a hair-band in an attempt to tame his overflowing locks and marched off to a press conference. The "Style" became a rage overnight and youngsters were seen aping it with elan in a few days. When we were at school it used to be a prank. To put a hair band on the head of some boy, you want to make a butt of jokes. For some time however this changed and Hair bands became Cool or rather Kewl.

That is the impact movie stars have in our lives. That is the reason millions are pumped into the publicity and advertising. They are walking and talking brands, who help sell products. The cost of saying the name of a product with a simple wave and smile goes into millions. People go crazy and rush to try out the new product. What I fail to understand is that why people bash these screen idols for earning money in the way of being brand ambassadors? What is so wrong in it? They are just cashing in on their image, which ironically has been created by the public. It is us who made them what they are, and if now they are using that to earn their bread and butter (*rather their luxury condos and Bentleys*), there is nothing illegal about it. Who in this world does not make a dollar where it is possible? They have the opportunity and they are milking it. If they do not, they would be called fools. The charisma is not everlasting. They know very well, that one day it shall fade away. So, they are making the most of it while they can. Just following *"Make Hay while the Sun shines"*. If we would be in their place, we would be doing nothing different. If you don't like someone up there reaping in the profits, do not put her/him up there. Simple.

Another point of painful interest in this glitzy world is about their relationships. People are obsessed about the supposed relationships, affairs, link-ups, break-ups and so on in the movie world. This cannot be blamed on the Indians alone, as it is a worldwide hobby. Unfair to say only women, so men and women obsessively follow the personal lives of their favorite and most hated celebrities. They assume that everything which is being broadcast and publicized is true. What they don't understand is, that all this is the part of a carefully cultivated and matured plan. A plan made by the public relationship manager of the said celebrity. Barring a few cases, we are never exposed to the truth, until the star herself or himself wishes for us to be exposed.

The so called scandals or candid photographs, or the leaked conversations are just a clever way to reach out to the audience. No one ever doubts the credibility of evidence, when it has supposedly been taken against the will of the accused. So that is what they do. When they wish to spread a message, they use means other than their own, to disseminate it amongst the crowd. This is an example of very smart media management. Next time you are being convinced of the hook up of a famous actress with a famous actor, do not be fooled. You are not so fortunate enough to be getting some inside information. It is just what is intended by both the parties. Apparently a movie premiere is nearby and the producer expects to earn some quick bucks by making his stars look more human.

They say that in the movie business it is ironical that a movie star gets paid mounds of fortune for performing probably the least strenuous task in the whole setup. It is really sad, that the 200 to sometimes 500 people involved and associated in the process of film making, are seldom heard about. True and believable. But, we should not forget that it is also an industry which is providing employment opportunity to these hundreds of workers with a creative turn of mind, who otherwise might have gone astray. If everyone entering the movie industry starts expecting to become a Tom Cruise or a Shah Rukh Khan, it won't be fair. Getting involved in the process and working is what is in our hands. Reaching to the top is something ordained by the Destiny. We may struggle against it, but can never win against Destiny. If it is written that someone will reach to the Top, they shall, no matter how many zig-zags or highs and lows they see. We should deliver what is in our powers and leave the rest to the higher ones.

Done the Unconventional all through the book, so let's carry on the tradition.

Let's call it CLOSURE instead of Epilogue. Sounds better, doesn't it?

CLOSURE

We come to the end of this volume. Spoke about a lot of things and yet, lots of things remain to be spoken about. We have just grazed a few critical and some not so critical topics. These sessions need to continue to achieve the real objective.

It was a real pleasure.

See you soon.

Au revoir.

ABOUT THE AUTHOR

Like any smart reader, we would like to know about the author who has penned this volume. Pulkit or Dr Pulkit Heera is someone who is a little difficult to describe. Professionally a Consultant Eye Surgeon, a reviewer for British and Indian Medical Journals and a speaker at Medicine conferences worldwide; Pulkit looks the part of a white collared professional, born in a family of dignified professionals. Perhaps he received the gift of a brilliant brain and sharp insight at birth, which enabled him to achieve a lot at a very young age. But, this is where the story just begins. The man is a raging storm of restless energy and thousand and one ideas. Since childhood, he has had an unquenchable thirst to learn everything possible, meet new people every day and a weakness for celebrations. He gets bored extremely easily and needs laughter and constant distractions in form of new hobbies to keep him alive. His life so far has been an attestation to the fact. The Doctor is- proficient in Indian instrumental classical music, western vocals, is an amateur Guitarist, loves lawn tennis, is an expert swimmer, sketches, is an actor and screenwriter in upcoming Bollywood movies, a mimic and a stage lover, a poet, a renowned orator, a fierce competitor in debates.................... and also an Author. Hira believes in laughing at and looking at everything through a different perspective, a perspective which embosses its beauty, humor and positivity. He revels in chucking the boring and breaking stereotypes. It may be safely said that the guy is a Jack of All and Master of few. The list sounds impressive, but has been assembled gradually due to the undying flame inside him, which constantly pushes him to grab and learn something new. In his own words- *"These virtues provide me with a sense of immense satisfaction and peace and help me reset and achieve a sense of being in this chaotic world with loud noises and disturbances"*.